WALK IN MY PAWS

WALK IN MY PAWS

An Anthology: Working Service Dogs

R. Rice

Walk in My Paws
An Anthology: Working Service Dogs

Copyright @ 2019

Library of Congress

ISBN: Print: 978-1687197009

Ebook (Amazon/Lulu) & NLS available

This book was printed in the
United States of America

Published Walk in My Paws
An Anthology: Working Service Dogs

October 2019, R. Rice

PRAISES IN *WALK IN MY PAWS*

*"Ramona Rice has put together an inspirational collection
of stories that highlight the amazing contribution of service dogs.
Walk in My Paws: An Anthology: Working Service Dogs fills an
important and educational niche in addition to answering pertinent
questions businesses and others may have. Everyone who has the
opportunity to read this book will find it well worth their time."*

**Jeanette Herbert, State of Utah First Lady
Governor's Mansion, Salt Lake City, Utah**

*"Beautiful, authentic stories about the beneficial and loving
companionship that exists between people and their service dogs.
Truly wonderful and memorable reading."*

**Lisa Nelson, Program Manager
Utah State Library, Salt Lake City, Utah**

*"Friendly and informative, these stories look at the
blessing that a young guide dog can be to someone that has had
vision taken away from them in the prime of their life. Experience
what happens when they are matched with their new partners that
are soon to become working guide dogs.*

*This book takes you into the minds and thoughts of 40
wanting recipients and as they share their expectations and hopes
of a brighter life with their new partner. Sometimes we all forget
the little things in life are the hardest to navigate and yet this is an
everyday reality for these amazing story tellers. I for one have
been touched by the insight of each journey."*

**Billy Vance, President,
Lions Club of Brentwood, California**

*"Profiles in Independence! A must-read book that tells the story of
more than three dozen people who acquire a disability and learn to
embrace it through their work with the animals who support them.
These stories reaffirm the resilience of humankind."*

**Patricia Yeager, Ph.D., CEO,
The Independence Center, Colorado Springs, Colorado**

DEDICATION

This book is dedicated to all working service dogs because they have given us their absolute all. We are the center of their universe; we are the focus of their love, faith, and trust.

THE BOND
Ronda Del Boccio

I was living on the edge,
Flailing in the gloom and dark,
Afraid to leap, afraid to fall,
Craving an uplifting spark,

Then, you came on padded feet,
Wagged your tail and licked my face,
Gave me purpose, gave me hope,
Filled my life with love and grace.

Love at my feet, love in the lead.
This wonderful dog is what I need,
To heal my heart, to find my way,
And ease my struggles every day.

When my heart is on the ground,
When I hurt too much to care,
You lift me up and show the way.
I'm not alone. You're always there.

Through the laughter, through the tears,
Through the cuddles, work and play,
Our loving bond will never break.
I give thanks for you each day.

Love at my feet, love in the lead.
This wonderful dog is what I need,
To heal my heart, to find my way,
And ease my struggles every day.

I love my dog.

CONTENTS

FOREWORD

Life can be extra challenging for people who need working service dogs to live healthily and enjoy their independence. The role of the working service dog is critical in their lives where the dog can guide, soothe, aid, and alert their humans and sometimes even save lives.

As we trek through many winding paths of emotions and experiences with our disabilities, the fear and insecurity continue. We are ready to step out of our comfort zone with our most trusted task-trained service dogs – despite our familiar foe. The foe is the people who are fraudulently representing their pets as a service dog. Their actions are relentless and unforgiving as it wages war upon our heart as they try to deny us the ability to experience the world around us.

Working service dogs are an extension of the person who has a disability. Imagine you're driving a car, a person distracted you by grabbing your hands from the steering wheel, and you crashed! Sadly, there are many disabled handlers injured from reckless and intentional distractions. Also, imagine if someone were to say, "Boy, I sure wish I had a wheelchair, walker, cane, crutch, oxygen tank, or prosthetic limb to take with me everywhere!" Wishing you had a service dog is exactly the same.

Walk in My Paws: An Anthology: Working Service Dogs book will take you to the most unfamiliar places – a collection of stories that will answer any questions. It will allow you to network, coordinate, and share their experiences to improve working service dog community's standard of living; and through unity, to conquer the foe. By picking up this book, you have shown your dedication, commitment, and passion for all working service dogs.

INTRODUCTION

Walk in My Paws: An Anthology: Working Service Dogs is a non-fiction book with multiple stories experiencing with a working service dog. A service dog, most wondrous, loyal, and faithful animal with a deeply encoded desire to attach to humans - they come alive when introduced to its new owner with a disability.

It's not just about teaching a service dog to perform specific tasks but to educate the human as well. The dog will be amazing when it has a person who really understands dogs, as well as understanding how to train and communicate effectively with them.

The book will challenge you to think differently about everything you thought you knew about working service dogs. Immerse yourself in each writer's beautiful, riveting, and often funny stories about such experiences. One valuable lesson is that there is a success within the great difficulty and countless obstacles, including the people misrepresenting their pets as a service dog. Regardless, each working service dog handler's hopes and dreams will be fulfilled with aspirations and with their steely determination. They will persevere.

ACKNOWLEDGMENTS

Walk in My Paws: An Anthology: Working Service Dogs is a collaborative effort of multiple writers who are handlers, trainers, instructors, puppy-raisers, and advocates. Many have come from different walks of life to share similar experiences in coping and adjusting with a service dog. These beautiful writers, most resilient and creative, share their humor and compassion for you to walk alongside them, and to gain insight into their struggles and triumphs.

Our immense gratitude to R. Rice, the mastermind behind the book project; she conceived the idea to create awareness about the public's misconceptions on task-trained service dogs. While she worked tirelessly with compiled stories, articles, and resources, she truly enjoyed working with all contributors in the book. She contributed her personal story, *We Must Go On!*, where her struggle is felt, alongside many other working service dog handlers, about the rise of fake service dogs.

R. Rice also created and published a book, *Walk in My Shoes: An Anthology on Usher Syndrome*. The book is a collection of 28 writers, including herself, impacted by Usher syndrome, the loss of both vision and hearing. She is often referred to as "Usher Warrior" by her colleagues as she hosted many significant events for the communities of the deaf, blind, deaf-blind, veterans, and service dogs.

R. Rice lives in Utah to enjoy her quality time with her self-accomplished children, Jason and Autumn; and Christa and Kelcee; and their amazingly funny and beautiful children, Jason, Max, Zoe, and Jett. She loves to travel to re-connect with her old friends from afar and near. Snuggling, with her current Golden

Retriever working service dog, Stormy, from The Seeing Eye, is always a bonus after a fulfilling day!

Randy Dewitt, *Walk in My Paws'* editor, is a native of Boston, Massachusetts. He has Usher syndrome, Type 1B, which means he is entirely deaf with progressive vision loss. His vision loss described as tunnel vision that potentially could shrink down to pinholes of light later in life.

Randy has advocated for deaf-blind rights and accessibility for ten years in Massachusetts. Randy has taught American Sign Language (ASL) classes for a local high school, local branch of the YMCA, and a senior citizen center. He edited R. Rice's first book, *Walk in My Shoes: An Anthology on Usher Syndrome.*

Randy has learned a lot about guide dogs and service animals as he worked with the stories in the book. He has gained many insights into these beautiful animals, and he hopes that others will learn as much from all the stories in this book as he has.

Dan Burgess, brother of Matt Burgess, founder of Freedom Fidos, created *Walk in My Paws'* book photos. Dan adopted his love for photography along with his loving wife, Bonnie. Together, they started a photography business, D&B Forever Photography. Their love and serving attitude in photography put their customers at ease, and the feedback from every single customer is the same; they have never had a photoshoot be so relaxed and friendly.

Currently, D & B Forever Photography is thriving with so many happy customers, each with a unique story. Running a business with technology experience into the photography business, running their website, and being a part of the Freedom Fidos' team is a blessing for them.

Zinia Mangleburg is an aspiring dentist who has had a lifelong passion for the arts, and for providing care to the underserved. She is currently working as a dental assistant while going through the dental school application process. She enjoys a variety of artistic pursuits including watercolor paintings of dogs and other subjects, quilting, realistic portraiture, and graphic design.

Zinia self-published an adult coloring-book called "Mindful Mandalas: Find Your Center" and is working on similar projects for the future

It is with much appreciation Zinia offered her expertise for *Walk in My Paws'* book cover designs, marketing sheet, and marketing video.

Aziza Rodriguez is a Home Health and Respite Care Provider and is passionate about disability rights and empowerment. She is committed to sharing her experience and guiding the next generation in realizing their dreams.

Aziza is a kind, compassionate, and selfless person yet very professional when she assisted in stories' editing and provided a comprehensive database of resources. She has contributed a personal tale, *Misadventure of Marna and Me.*

Janet Ingber lives in New York City, New York with her husband, Frank, and her guide dog, Pete. She has a 23-year-old daughter, Jill, who resides in Washington, D.C.

Janet has a Bachelor of Arts degree from Queens College, (CUNY), in Psychology/Sociology and a master's degree in Music Therapy from New York University. Janet has written numerous articles for the American Foundation for the Blind's (AFB) AccessWorld. She has also written for National Braille Press and American Printing House for the Blind. Janet is also a music therapist and works with adults who have developmental disabilities.

Janet contributed two chapters: *Training at Home with Freedom Guide Dogs for the Blind* and *Tips for Getting a Guide Dog* and provided valuable input along the way for the book's Resources and Tips pages.

Ronda Del Boccio is an author of many books, articles, and poems, and generously wrote a poem, *THE BOND*, for the Dedication page. Ronda is known for her sweet disposition and humorous personality. She contributed an entertaining chapter, *Meeting My Juno*.

Beth Meador wrote a poem for R. Rice in her chapter, *My Guide Dog, My Friend* to ease her heart-wrenching pain after the loss of her first guide dog, Sabrina. Beth has *retinitis pigmentosa* with less than 2 degrees of vision left. She prided herself as an extraordinary artist to bring smiles to those in emotional pain. She is loved by many from afar and near for her acts of kindness.

It is with appreciation to all authors in the book to share their personal experiences. Internally challenging and rewarding that makes *Walk in My Paws* book a touching, heartfelt memoir of their journeys with their working service dogs. Without experiences and support from these authors, this book would not exist.

Lastly, Cheryl Wilcox is a role model and mentor to many. She is admired for her creativity and inventiveness in her writing skill, personally and professionally.

In appreciation of all dogs' trainers, instructors, advocates, and puppy-raisers for their hard work and support. Cheryl wrote this beautiful poem - Just for you:

UNSUNG HEROES

You dedicate your life to
Helping others succeed

Thinking little of yourself…
Only of those in need.

You spend countless hours
Helping each of us through
A struggle here and there
But I see the unsung hero in you.

With patience and understanding
You helped me find my way
You truly listened to me
Knowing the words, I did not say.

You helped me obtain the equipment,
skills, and training I need to survive
You think of it as just your job…
But I know heroes are still alive.

You continue to help me and
others for as long as it takes.
You think it isn't much
But what a difference it makes!

There are no adequate words and
A simple thanks will never do
But with heartfelt recognition we see
The unsung hero in each of you.

An effort to raise awareness and to change the public's misconceptions about highly task-trained service dogs' roles - R. Rice donates 100% royalties from the *Walk in My Paws: An Anthology: Working Service Dogs* book to Freedom Fidos, a non-profit organization based in Columbus, Georgia. The effort is to support their incredible program by transforming rescued shelter dogs into highly task-trained working service dogs for disabled veterans and first responders at no cost to the recipient.

To learn more and support Freedom Fidos' organization - www.freedomfidos.org

PART 1

THE STRENGTH OF INDEPENDENCE AND EMPOWERMENT

CHAPTER 1

TWO MIRACLES
WORKING TOGETHER

Bracha Ben-Avraham

Noah Braun, co-founder, and director of the Israel Guide Dog Center for the Blind remarked: "We take the dog and the harness and the training, and although we're not magicians, we create a miracle." I think that every guide dog team consists of two miracles. The first is the dog transformed from a playful puppy into a trustworthy, faithful companion capable of guiding us safely down the street. The second is the independence, confidence, and empowerment that guide dogs bring into our lives. That miracle happened for me eight years ago when I received my first guide dog from the Israel Guide Dog Center for the Blind.

I was born 12 weeks prematurely and placed in intensive neonatal care in an incubator like many such babies. I ended up with a condition known as *retinopathy of prematurity* (ROP) but was one of the lucky children to be left with some remaining vision. I grew up in the United States and was integrated into the mainstream educational system.

My parents encouraged me to be independent and to overcome my disability. Partially sighted people often have a difficult time finding their place and identity. Unlike people with total blindness, the extent of our limitations and abilities is often unclear to us and those around us. I had a confused identity and sat on the fence between two worlds: the blind and the sighted. My way of dealing with this was to deny the existence of my visual impairment, and I developed sophisticated methods of hiding it from others. I often succeeded in covering up my disability, but my efforts required a lot of time and energy.

When I was ten, I began attending a summer camp that was sponsored by a Jewish and Zionist youth movement. For the first time, my friends accepted me. I could sing, play the guitar, and dance as well as everyone else, and they treated me as an equal. It was there that I felt self-confident and happy. I joined the leadership training program and became a camp counselor.

When I turned 18, I decided to leave home to study and live in Israel. I was determined to become a kindergarten teacher and join a kibbutz. However, I began to encounter obstacles and prejudices. To my dismay, people told me that I could not be a teacher because of my visual disability and advised me to seek a different profession. I insisted on pursuing my goal and became a kindergarten teacher. I then joined a kibbutz on Israel's northern border, married, and raised my two children. I worked in childcare and taught kindergarten.

Later, I left teaching and became a farmer. Many members of the kibbutz felt that I would not be able to do agricultural work because of my visual disability, but once again, I insisted on setting my own limits. I planted and cultivated fruit trees, drove tractors, weeded the cotton, picked oranges, and did everything that my fellow kibbutzniks did.

My strategy of living my life as a sighted person suddenly fell apart in my late 30s. I suddenly lost all the vision in one eye and experienced a sharp decline in my vision in the other. I began to realize that I needed to come to terms with my disability. Reluctantly, I had to leave the world of the sighted behind and join the world of the blind.

My deteriorating vision began to affect my mobility. I received training with a cane, but I was ashamed to take it out of my bag and use it because I did not want people in the street to know that I couldn't see. When I went out with friends, they began to continually warn me of stairs, poles, and other obstacles that I could not see. I was going down the path that I had been fighting against all my life; Instead of remaining independent, I was depending on others. I was no longer overcoming my visual disability. It was overcoming me.

I longed to regain my independence and to get control of my life again. The solution, of course, was evident. I needed to get a guide dog. In 2009, I made one of the best decisions I have ever made: I called the Israel Guide Dog Center and applied for a guide dog.

Many of us experience conflicts and dilemmas when making a crucial decision about getting a guide dog. My most significant battle was admitting that I no longer had sufficient vision to get around safely. But, I loathed using a white cane so much that I was willing to take that final step of adopting a guide dog and entering the world of the blind.

In the fall of 2009, I attended a three-day evaluation course at the Israel Guide Dog Center for the Blind. The course allows the instructors and the candidate to assess whether or not a guide dog is the best solution for attaining safe mobility. During the course, my mobility and orientation skills evaluated, I walked with a dog that had nearly completed its training. Throughout the course, I was fearful I had "too much vision" to have a guide dog and that I would be told to come back in the future if my vision worsened. But, when the instructor and I met, I was told that I would continue with the application process! I was placed on the waiting list to receive a dog!

I returned home happy and settled down for what I expected to be a waiting period of several months. After one month, and with my delight, I was invited to attend the training course, and I received my first guide dog, Suki – a stunningly beautiful white Golden Retriever.

The training course at the Israel Guide Dog Center is a two-and-a-half-week course with a set structure and specific goals. Students live on the pastoral campus located at the Beit Oved junction, 20 minutes south of Tel Aviv. Courses include up to six participants and are conducted by one or two instructors depending upon the size of the course. Clients are blind or visually impaired Israelis who come from a wide variety of religious and ethnic backgrounds: Jews, Muslims, Christians, new immigrants, and disabled veterans. Most clients attend on-campus courses, but domiciliary courses are given to people who require individual instruction such as deaf-blind clients or for new mothers who cannot leave home.

Learning to use a guide dog when you have some remaining vision has unique challenges. You must learn to use your vision wisely while relinquishing control to the dog. It is a question of placing trust in your dog, knowing that it will do its job. I wanted to learn to trust my dog without using my remaining vision and did some of the walks on the course blindfolded. I vividly remember standing on a dark city street in a nearby town during a nighttime walk, afraid to proceed. Suddenly, I realized that I could trust this beautiful dog to guide me through the dark. I gave my dog the command "Kadima" which means "forward" in Hebrew and navigated the dark street!

After I returned home with Suki, my life changed completely. I no longer feel the need to hide the fact that I am visually impaired. Walking with a guide dog makes my identity clear to others as well as to me. My guide dog enables me to accept my status as a visually impaired person. I was ashamed to walk with a white cane. Now, I am proud to walk down the street with my guide dog.

Suki is no longer with me, but I now have Dinka, my second guide dog, a beautiful Labrador-Golden Retriever cross. I work at the Israel Guide Dog Center for the Blind in fundraising and marketing. My work involves traveling and speaking to school children, donors, and supporters in Israel, the United States, and Canada. Great Britain remained inaccessible to guide dog handlers for many years because of the quarantine laws. In 2012, the laws were eliminated, and Dinka and I became the first guide dog team to enter Great Britain.

Dinka is my constant companion. She is a reminder of who I am and of the independent person I want to be. I am pleased with her, excited of the empowerment that she gives me, and proud to be part of the guide dog school that has changed my life.

About the Israel Guide Dog Center for the Blind

The Israel Guide Dog Center for the Blind is a member of the International Guide Dog Federation and is the only certified guide dog school in the Middle East. Before its establishment in 1992, Israelis who wanted a guide dog had to travel abroad to the U.S. or Great Britain to receive a guide dog. They returned home with a dog that only understood commands in English that were unaccustomed to the Israeli climate and environment and follow-up or aftercare were unavailable.

The center has created close to 600 guide dog-teams in the past 25 years. Clients include Israelis from all religious and ethnic backgrounds, new immigrants, and disabled veterans. The center is located south of Tel Aviv and has a purpose-built campus, kennels, puppy breeding center, and training grounds.

The cost of raising, training each dog and instructing each client is approximately $30,000. Israel Guide Dog Center for the Blind provides guide dogs, training, and services free of charge. The school is a non-profit organization, and the government funds 5% of creating each guide dog partnership. The remainder comes from contributions from friends and supporters in Israel and abroad. They give Guide dog users in Israel a monthly government stipend that covers the costs of food and veterinary expenses. It makes it possible for anyone who needs a guide dog to receive one regardless of their financial situation.

The center creates about 35 guide dog-teams each year and plans to increase that number to 50. All puppies are bred from the center's breeding stock and are puppy raised by more than 70 puppy walkers, many of whom are university students. Dogs that do not qualify as guide dogs are given to families with a child or adult with special needs. These dogs do not receive any specialized training but are, nevertheless, valuable dogs that serve as faithful companions.

Since 2009, the center has used the clicker technique of positive reinforcement to train guide dogs. The method has proven to be hugely successful. Dogs complete training in a shorter period, are highly motivated, and learn quickly. During the training course, guide dog handlers are taught to use a clicker to train their dogs to locate essential objects such as an empty bench, ATM, the button at a stoplight crossing, or a storefront.

Guide Dogs in Israel

Working with a guide dog in Israel is challenging. Sidewalks are often narrow and filled with obstacles; illegally parked cars and motorcycles, trees, lamp posts, and street furniture. Electric bicycles whiz by and cannot be heard and are hazardous to everyone. The climate in Israel is sweltering in the summer, and temperatures climb to the upper 90s or higher. Sidewalks and pavements become burning hot in the noon-day sun, and guide dog handlers are encouraged to use protective shoes the dogs' paws. It is essential to carry a bottle of water and a portable drinking bowl when taking a guide dog outside during the summer.

Accessibility legislation has existed in Israel since 1991. The law allows guide dog handlers to enter all public domains and to use public transport. Recent amendments to the original legislation also permit access to puppy-walkers and guide dog trainers with dogs in training.

Israel is a multi-cultural and multi-religious country, and many people still harbor deep-seated cultural and religious prejudices against dogs. Islam considers dogs to be impure animals and forbids people to have contact with them, and Orthodox Jews are reluctant to keep dogs in their homes. Consequently, despite legislation, guide dog handlers still encounter resistance from taxi drivers, bus drivers, and business owners who refuse to obey the law. The Israel Guide Dog Center for the Blind is continuously working together with other organizations to increase public awareness and to ensure that the accessibility law is enforced.

We hope soon that blind and visually impaired Israelis of all religious and cultural backgrounds will overcome their prejudices and will be able to enjoy the many advantages that guide dogs have to offer.

This chapter is dedicated to my faithful guide dogs, Suki and Dinka, and to all the guide dogs who will be with me in the future.

CHAPTER 2

INTRIGUE: MY FAVORITE RUNNING BUDDY

Brian Switzer

My name is Brian Switzer; I am 27 years old, and I am a marathoner. I have run the Boston Marathon twice. I have run the Equinox Marathon in Alaska, the Wings for Life World Run in Munich, and I ran on the first team of all blind and visually impaired athletes to complete a Ragnar Relay Ultra. I am a graduate student at Suffolk University. I study Ethics and Public Policy with a focus on justice as it relates to disability. I am also deafblind with a significant hearing loss and no functional vision. I can see the light, but when I walk outside, everything goes to a blurry white, and when I go inside, everything goes to a very dark black. When I knew I was going blind at the age of 11 I wanted a guide dog. Those blind people with guide dogs always looked so sophisticated with their dark shades being guided down the street by a huge and confident German Shepherd. Now I navigate my surroundings with the help of my own guide dog; a Labrador Retriever named Intrigue.

Before getting Intrigue, I traveled between my house and school using a long cane. The commute would take me almost two hours in each direction. There is no available paratransit service in my town so the most affordable way to get to school is to ride an Uber, two trains, and then walk over to the school. I would get a horrible anxiety every time before leaving the house. The stress of anxiety developed as a result of the fear of getting lost. I passed my orientation and mobility lessons with flying colors, but I would always get anxious. I never showed it, though. Orientation and mobility instructors will tell you to travel with confidence.

Thanks to Intrigue's speed, the daunting two-hour commute is closer to an hour and a half. I don't have the same anxiety that I used to. Part of it is that Intrigue is really good at memorizing routes. When I travel to school, I no longer have to give her commands. She will find and point out each non-visual landmark on her own. The other part of it is that I am less reliant on my hearing. A guide dog can point out a door without you having to listen for it. When you have significant hearing loss, listening out for objects, such as doors, can be overwhelming and exhausting. I still get lost from time to time on newer routes. However, I no longer have that fear of getting lost. At least when you get lost with a guide dog, you have a furry friend to keep you company.

Intrigue is so good at her job that she can memorize whole routes. One of my favorite places to go with her is a place near my house called Borderland State Park. We often hike it with friends. When I went on my first date with my girlfriend, we decided to hike Borderland. It is a pleasant place to walk around and talk. As a blind person, it is tough to go on dates with people with sight. You never know what kind of preconceived notions of blindness they hold. Hollywood depictions of blindness are not very accurate. My girlfriend had only been to Borderland once before, and she did not know the paths. I reassured her that Intrigue knew the whole route. I am sure it was not very reassuring, but she agreed to hike it with us. Intrigue guided the two of us the entire three-mile loop from start to finish. Intrigue and my skill at working together must have impressed her. She agreed to go on a second date with me after that.

One time, I hit my eye badly on a wooden chest. I had leaned over without first extending out my hands to protect my face, which is a big no-no in the blind community. When you cannot see, it is easy to hit your eye on things. Sighted people have a natural defense system against injuring their eyes. It's called their vision. The impact made me feel dizzy, and I had to sit down on the floor. My guide dog came over and laid down next to me until I had recovered a little bit. While it not necessarily her role to do so, she does comfort me from time to time.

My professors enjoy having Intrigue in class. She is quiet and hangs out on the floor out of the way of foot traffic. Now and then, she will interject into a conversation. One day, my professor was talking about the political theory of Edmund Burke. Intrigue let out a perfectly timed moan. My professor remarked that Intrigue disagreed with Burke's argument. We all had a good laugh. Everyone says how intelligent guide dogs are. Who knew they were smart enough to criticize Burke's political theory?

One time I left her alone while I ran on a treadmill. I lost a bunch of bananas. I lost not one, not two, not even three, but nine whole bananas. There was no trace that there ever were any bananas. Knowing that I was preoccupied, she had jumped up onto the counter to grab a snack. I did ultimately find the bananas a day later, and they passed through her system just fine.

The most fun activity to do with Intrigue is playing with her. As a blind person, I am always trying to find her toys. She has more toys than any dog I know, yet, I can never find them around the house. Her favorite game is fetching. However, the balls have a mind of their own. When I throw them, they end up bouncing off the walls or landing in places high up where Intrigue cannot reach. Her favorite time of day to play a rousing game of fetch is when the house is all quiet. The downside is that the only time the house is ever quiet is when people are sleeping or when my baby niece is taking a nap.

I applied to several guide dog schools, but my goal was to always get into Guiding Eyes for the Blind. The majority of my friends with guide dogs received theirs at Guiding Eyes. Guiding Eyes is known for their commitment to clients. After receiving a dog, they will still advise working with the dog or fly out to a client's home if a client faces a significant obstacle in working with the dog. They also offer a stipend for medical bills for the dogs. Their commitment is not just training guide dogs, but to train both handlers and guide dogs to work as a team to achieve mobility for the blind individual.

Guiding Eyes for the Blind based in Yorktown Heights, New York. They have a second location in White Plains, New York, where students go to complete part of their training. They are revered as the first school to use positive reinforcement training with their guide dogs. It means that the dogs enjoy their work. They enjoy it since they are rewarded with a treat or positive praise from their handler. They are also using their brains to problem-solve. To a guide dog, their work is a game. They find a landmark and receive a treat. Intrigue is a highly intelligent and active dog. Her job allows her to use her mind and get more exercise than a typical dog. She would never have survived as a pet who stayed home all day.

When a student is accepted by Guiding Eyes, he or she flies out, rides the train, or drives out to Yorktown Heights. There, you stay in the dorms for three weeks. The three-week training is primarily for you, as the handler. At this point, the dogs have completed two years of training successfully and passed all required tests to become a guide dog. First, the trainers at Guiding Eyes observe your ability to travel around. Then, they match you with a suitable dog and observe how well you two fit together. The crucial criteria for matching a dog to a handler is whether the two walks roughly at the same pace. After this, the training for the handler begins. They teach you all the commands, how to rework problems, and the rules and regulations around guide dogs. Guiding Eyes' training will put you in every imaginable situation. They drive you out to the White Plains location where they put you and your dog on a train, on escalators, on stairs, on a bus, in a mall, in a store, down a dirt road, through revolving doors, and more. You name it. They put you in that situation. This way, when you go home, you are ready for every situational setting you and your dog will encounter.

Guiding Eyes for the Blind breeds and trains Labrador Retrievers and German Shepherds. Intrigue herself is a Labrador Retriever. However, she does not look like a typical Labrador Retriever breed because she is black with tan markings above her eyebrows, on her paws, and under her belly. She gets confused a lot for a Rottweiler or a German Shepherd. The black and tan is a recessive trait. Her father is a yellow Labrador, and her mother is a black Labrador. Her litter is primarily made up of black Labradors except for her and her black and tan brother, Idaho. The American Kennel Association prohibits black and tan Labradors from being shown in the ring. The American Kennel Association decides and highlights a lot of the standards of various dog breeds. Most breeders will breed this trait out of their genetic lines. They opt for more "pure" genetic lines, where the dogs only come out with the standard yellow and black coloring. Guiding Eyes does not. They breed dogs to be service dogs, so they keep the dogs with the black and tan trait. These dogs are equally gifted at being guide dogs as their yellow and black siblings.

Along with her black and tan markings, Intrigue is a unique dog in a second way. She is one of about ten official running guide dogs in the United States. Guiding Eyes for the Blind hosts the only official running guide dog program in the U.S. The dogs and their handlers go through training to learn how to run together. I traveled down to Yorktown Heights to complete a week-long training regimen with Intrigue. We went running twice a day while being coached along the way. Imagine not being able to see. Now, imagine not being able to see while putting your whole trust in the paws of a dog. Again, imagine doing all of that while running on dirt paths weaving through the woods. It is an exhilarating experience. It is also a freeing one. I can go out for a run on my own schedule. Running with my guide dog allows for more independence. With a guide dog, I am in control of the pace, where we decide to run, and how far we want to go (of course, you cannot go any further than the dog wants to).

When Intrigue runs with me, she wears a different harness. Her running harness allows her to move about more freely than her work harness. The work handle on the harness is called an ergonomic handle. An ergonomic handle is placed at a slant so that the handler's hand is more comfortably situated. The ergonomic handle also pushes the handler a bit more away from the dog. This allows the dog a little more space when the two are running together. The running harness is hand made at Guiding Eyes, and they are currently working with M.I.T. to develop a new generation of guide dog harnesses that can be utilized both for regular guide work and for running. For my part, I wear a vest that is written as "Blind" in large-sized letters. It informs the public that a blind person is about to run past them. As you can imagine, the general public is not familiar seeing blind people with guide dogs sprinting down the sidewalk directly at them.

Intrigue loves to run; she is a small dog with a short stride. She made up for her short pace by being quick in her step as if she is "scurrying." Intrigue can run about four miles at a slow speed. As a marathoner, I still rely on people to guide me on the longer runs. Intrigue is currently helping me to train for the New York City Marathon and the Beantown Marathon.

It is easy to say that my guide dog has brought me a lot of joy and newfound independence that I would not be able to appreciate without her. She has been with me through thick and thin. She is my running buddy and my guide to school. Most of all, she is my best friend.

CHAPTER 3

MASTERS OF TRANSIENCE

George Stern

The homey susurrus of Lubbock's Preston International airport in Texas was interrupted by a screeching that sounded like a convention of jeopardy buzzers decrying the absolute wrong answer ever given. It went on, and on, and on... Finally, inaudible to me but relayed by a fellow passenger, the announcement came through that the luggage carousel was broken, and we should proceed across the airport to an alternative baggage claim. Wrong answer. Vale, my black Labrador-Golden Retriever cross dog guide, stood placidly during all this commotion and snapped a brisk right pivot with me to begin our walk to the new baggage claim. This right turn is important. They instruct you minutely in such things, or at least The Seeing Eye in Morristown, New Jersey, does; the essential elements of right and left turns for two bodies attempting to move as one. As I recall, the right turn was a choreographed mini-dance of "right leg back and turning out, so; right hand, shoulders, and head indicating right, so; left hand on the harness angling just so..." It has to be "as I recall", because six years on, turns never come in for conscious, step-by-step consideration anymore. We just turn.

The trip to the new carousel was a dreamy drift on the cusp of a wave of other migrating passengers, Vale settling into a dead-level pace that kept us off the heels of those in front and off the toes of those behind. Only when I started to sense the disintegration of our wave, people falling away from us did hesitation come through the harness; a slight swivel of the head, a slight slackening of stride that cued me to ask of my companions if we were almost there. We were.

Vale's disciplined focus at this moment was a relief and a reminder. We'd just spent a whirlwind weekend in Austin, Texas, where everything from his guiding work to his bowels seemed just a bit off; heck, he was even exhibiting stage fright at one point as I sat on a panel. Here, though, in the ultimate flux space that is an airport, Vale seemed to regain his calm, dignified, sure self. It figures; from the day I got him, I've never flown less than thrice per year. We've had eight flights already, seven months into 2017, with more on the horizon. And, Vale loves it. I feel it in his pinpoint alert towards the jetway at the chime of a call button; in his strut along the jetway, boarding or disembarking; in his whiplash reactions as we parallel one impressed skycap or another through swirling chaos to make a connection. Even as he insists on more frequent toilet breaks – (he's ten years old now) – his flying bladder is iron, holding steady for fifteen-hour flying days.

In preparation, diligent research and strict rule-following were the guarantors of a successful handler-guide team, Vale and I shouldn't have worked out. Not at all. I'm often bemused, from my vantage as an administrator of the Guide Dog Handlers' Network Facebook group, to see the degree to which prospective handlers preoccupy themselves with getting the first dog; daily countdowns like Harry Potter anticipating Hogwarts; what-if and how-should questions; questions about food, toys, the ownership/discipline/graduate support policies of different guide schools; worries about guides interacting with family and pets. My overriding preoccupation in the dying days of spring 2011 when I flew to my class at The Seeing Eye was whether or not my application to Texas Tech University had been accepted, or should I start planning for a full-time career in competitive Brazilian Jiu-jitsu, and would I have a house to return to. The answers, respectively: yes, no, and temporarily. I returned home with Vale in June, got accepted to Texas Tech in July, and went home to see my family being evicted. That was our start. They warned us against taking moving walkways; we wandered accidentally onto one en-route back from a wedding in San Diego, California, mere weeks later. Suggestions were given about acclimatization, so many months to accustom your guide to your surrounds; Vale and I stayed in four different states, four different cities, and seven separate residences in four months in our first year. I was lucky in that Vale came to me older: he was four-years-old, a reissue who knew his stuff. I was fortunate in being matched with a smart, calm, quiet lover of novelty and challenge, free-form learning and essential purposes; a fellow master of transience.

On June 7, 2019, Vale has officially retired, and I thought I knew what I'd miss: the quiet presence of mere finger snap away, a warm inconvenience right in my spot on the bed, the ease of airport travel with a guide dog. Every silent step taken in this apartment furnishes yet more things: the clatters of ears and tail shaken, the soft scuff of paws on the carpet, the muted thump of his elbows hitting the floor when he plunks down. As I pass one corner, I'm surprised not to feel the familiar crumple-clutter of rubber food, and water bowl knocked askew; the joy at finding a strap poop bag in a pocket gutters unmoored, unstructured, the once-significant time windows from 5:00-7:00 a.m., 10:00-12:00 a.m., 5:00-7:00 p.m., and 9:00-10:00 p.m. suddenly undifferentiable from any other slice of the day. I feel unmoored, bereft of the grounding confidence and competence conferred by the peculiar dependence and trust of a dog guide.

On our last morning together, I made his leash long one last time, knelt in the New Hampshire spring mud and cried, struggling to fit inadequate words around the scope of my thanks. The tears fit better than any words could. What words, after all, could encompass eight years of service more faithful, more selfless, more forgiving, and understanding than any God's? What words could encompass starving together, being lost, and finding our way together, being hopeless and finding joy, the periods of frenetic travel and mind-numbing stagnation…..what words? None. Thank you, Seeing Eye, for the gift of an unparalleled partner. Thank you for letting me own him fully and unconditionally. Thank you for giving Vale and me such a solid foundation of knowledge and training to work from, then trusting us to do so. Vale is with my girlfriend, Danielle's family in Manchester, New Hampshire, now.

Here's hoping you get to see at least one more of those New England winters you seem to enjoy so much, Vale, Sir Boy. I dedicate this story to you.

CHAPTER 4

WE MUST GO ON!

R. Rice

For many years, it has been a passion of mine to create an inspirational book of multiple stories about working service dogs. It's vital to educate the public to be more aware, respectful, and understanding of service dogs' roles and the long-standing of ADA's law.

It has never been my place to police anyone about their animals in public places. However, when pet dogs who bark at working service dogs, charge/lunge toward them, or worse – attack them – it may cause a disabled person to fall, feel personally threatened, or in need to protect their service dog – possibly incurring injury to oneself or their dog in the melee. As a result of an attack, a service dog may become too fearful to continue working and be forced to retire.

Since 2005, there has been a significant rise with people misrepresenting their pets as working service dogs. Many handlers and trainers are often asked, "Where can I get a vest so I can take my pet everywhere with me?" Purchasing a vest or putting a 'service dog' identification badge on a pet dog does not make it a working service dog. It makes it a fraud.

Sadly, some individuals flout the laws designed to protect the rights of people with disabilities. There are dogs not cut out to be service dogs. Unknowingly or blatantly, people are deciding their pets are qualified working service animals. It causes many businesses to doubt disabled handlers with their working service dogs.

An important note: Veterans and non-veterans with *traumatic brain injury* or *Post Traumatic Stress Disorder (PTSD)* are especially vulnerable in public places. They are most likely to be questioned by business employees about their service dogs. They may have their symptoms triggered or worsened by such questioning. The questioning can also cause undue attention and humiliation.

My service dog, Stormy, is trained to perform specific tasks for a particular disability of mine. I am a deaf-blind person. His job is to guide me safely everywhere; unfortunately, he was attacked twice, but he bounced back as if he was saying, "Come, mum, we must go on!"

Whatever their intentions, people who wish to take their pets into places of public accommodation under the guise of service dog status must consider the legal and social consequences. Hopefully, they will choose instead to respect the rights of people with disabilities.

Stormy was a tremendous help to me while I dealt with a double mastectomy and aggressive chemotherapy treatments. For more than two years, I was a miserable patient with so many uncontrollable side effects from prescribed medications. Stormy is a fast walker and energetic when working, but he noticed the pain and difficulty of mine with high fevers, frequent infections, shivering, dehydration, nausea, emergency room trips, and without an additional training, he has helped me by walking slower for me to catch my breaths and guided me to wheelchair ramps so I wouldn't lose my balance. He often looked over his shoulder to see me as if he's saying, "You ok, mum?" He often placed his body on top of mine to keep me from shivering violently and calmed me during my nausea spells. He picked up my dropped items to hand them to me so I wouldn't have to bend down with my aching bones. He was amazing! He still is!

People would say, "It's just a dog." Hm, so not true. Stormy is not "just a dog." He was trained to guide me, love me, and protect me. He saved my life – literally. He's definitely more than "just a dog" because he's my everything! I value his presence, I appreciate his calmness, I respect his job, and I simply adore him for all he's doing!

For my first guide dog, Sabrina, my love. A poem written by Beth Meador.

MY GUIDE DOG, MY FRIEND

I bonded with you from the beginning
The match must have come from above
You were more than just a guide dog
You were my heart, my life, my love

We walked the streets together
You were constantly by my side
You gave me my independence
In a world where I wanted to hide

We traveled together through the years
In sunshine, rain and snow
Over the sidewalks and through the stores
My confidence continued to grow

You kept me safe and led the way
Constant and true to the end
A loyal servant all the way
My companion, My guide dog,

MY FRIEND

Although I had to say goodbye
My heart was broken through
I'm blessed to have had you in my life
Sabrina, I'll always love you

To show support for all deserving working service dogs through ADI (Assistance Dog International) by clicking this link: http://assistancedoginternational.org/access-and-laws/adi-guide-to-assistance-dog-law. Use the guidelines to educate your friends, family, and community leaders when discussing service dog fraud and the problem it has caused.

A message, "We must go on!" is a comforting motivation from my dog to me and I would like to extend that onto you. Do NOT quit your freedom – think of life's broader goals – the goals of surviving, avoiding injury, finding happiness, and living in accordance with our personal values among people whom we respect and who respect us.

Having independence and freedom taken from me by people who are misrepresenting a pet as a service dog, it's not only illegal, but it is without a moral compass.

As a creator *of Walk in My Paws: An Anthology: Working Service Dogs* and *Walk in My Shoes: An Anthology on Usher Syndrome* I dedicate this chapter to both of my amazing seeing-eye dogs, Sabrina (2002-2012) and Stormy (2014 -present) from The Seeing Eye, Inc., Morristown, New Jersey. Without them by my side, I would not have succeeded in many things independently. Thank you both, my loves!

PART 2

THROUGH OUR EYES

CHAPTER 5

PRESCHOOL & PUPPY RAISERS

Holly Bonner

I thought the sudden snowstorm that Saturday morning was nature's way of telling me I did not have to go tour preschools for my almost four-year-old daughter. My husband, on the other hand, was hell-bent on not letting a little snow get in our way. We had arranged for babysitting with my in-laws and headed out the door that morning.

"Goodbye, Mama," my daughter shouted as I grabbed my purse, "I hope you have fun looking at my new school."

I wanted to throw up. Literally. Even with September almost nine months away, the thought of my "baby" leaving me every day, entrusting her safety to strangers, filled my mind with dread. When we finally found ourselves sitting in the parking lot that snowy January morning, my husband assured me we were doing the right thing. Frances, my guide dog, snuck her head behind the back seat and licked my ear. I said, "Let's go, girl." And with that, she hopped out of the car, and I snapped the leather handle into the harness. "Forward, Franny." There was no turning back now.

The weather had deterred a lot of people from attending the open house that morning, placing more unwanted attention on my husband and I, the obviously nervous blind mother and her snow-covered guide dog. When we entered into what could quite possibly be my daughter's classroom, I felt as though I was going to have a panic attack. All I could see were clotheslines with papers hanging from them, the silhouette of a wooden toy kitchen and endless rows of tiny desks. My eyesight prevented me from seeing any further, and the negative self-talk commenced in my head:

How are you going to get her here every day?
What if the kids pick on her because I'm blind?
Am I going to be able to volunteer in the classroom?
Will the teacher...

My last thought was interrupted because Frances decided to intercede. My beautiful, furry partner pressed her body close to mine. Franny lifted her head and looked up at me, as if to say, "Hey, Mom, we've got this. You and me. We've got this." That's when I thought of you, her puppy-raisers, and how much your immense sacrifice has impacted my family.

Puppy-raisers like yourselves play such an integral role in preparing these remarkable dogs to be our guides. I want you to know that I think of your sacrifice during times like these. When I feel the foreboding sense of doubt in my abilities to live an independent life, it gives me the strength to consider how you and your family volunteered to foster an adorable, cuddly puppy.

No one asked or forced you to do the job, and you knew it was going to be hard, and you were committed.

As Frances' raisers, you looked after her. You cared for her. Your selfless devotion carefully laid the foundation for her training. For close to a year, you kept and loved the dog fate had decided would come to me, all the while knowing that one day you would say good-bye, perhaps wondering if you would ever see her again.

I don't pretend to know why you and your family chose to make such a heart-wrenching sacrifice. I can only tell you what that sacrifice has provided for me as a wife and mother of two little girls.

My husband no longer worries when I leave the house alone. Fears about me falling or getting lost are a distant memory now that I have Franny by my side. I can pick up that container of strawberries and bushel of bananas at the grocery store 14 blocks from my home – alone. I can attend work functions without loading two kids into car seats and my spouse chauffeuring me. I can even walk to Starbucks and get a cup of hot chocolate by myself, 20 minutes of mom-free time, where I get that much-needed break that so often saves my sanity. Having Frances has given me that. You have given me that.

My daughters, ages two and three, love that yellow Labrador as much as any child could ever love a dog. They hug her, play dress-up with her, invite her to tea parties. All the while, "St. Frances" puts up with being squeezed, shoved, and adorned with pearls and tiaras. When my daughters wake up every morning Frances circles each of them, her tail intently wagging as she sniffs, licks and showers them with affection. While I will attribute some of her temperament to Guiding Eyes for the Blind's fantastic breeding program, I would be remiss if I did not give your family credit for part of the calmness and gentleness in her demeanor. Undoubtedly, in her training, you must have had our Franny around children because she has happily assumed her role as a surrogate mother for my daughters.

There is a piece of your family that beats within the heart of my dog. I feel it every single day when I grip Frances' harness. I think of you every time I make it to the mailbox or find that elusive flight of stairs. I think of you on days it rains or snows, and I'm still able to make it to that doctor's appointment without canceling. There are times when I thought of you when I was able to find the ladies' room with my little girl who "really had to go." A part of you is with us on every single route daily.

With preschool fast approaching, maybe you can relate to the anxiety I'm having over letting go of my little girl. It must be very similar to how your family felt the day you let go of Frances, so another person you never met could benefit from her training.

I want you to know this amazing creature we both have grown to love is more than just my guide dog. Frances is more than a mobility tool. She has also become my partner, my confidant, and my friend in blindness. Every day, Frances gives me confidence, self-assurance, and a level of independence I had only dreamed possible. So, thank you to Frances' puppy-raisers and to Guiding Eyes for the Blind, for giving this mother of two my four-legged angel, complete with a leather harness.

With Franny by my side, I know I'll be able to navigate preschool. After all, "We've got this."

This story is dedicated to the many unsung heroes in the world of guide dogs – the selfless puppy-raisers. Thank you for opening your homes and your hearts to the beautiful animals who become our partners. We are forever in your debt.

CHAPTER 6

NAVIGATING LIFE
WITH MY DOG BY MY SIDE

Annie Donnell

My name is Annie Donnell, and I just completed my senior year at Belmont University in Nashville, Tennessee, where I majored in Communication Studies with a minor in Education. On June 5, 2016, I received my first guide dog from Guide Dogs for the Blind (GDB) in Oregon. My guide dog, Hikari, is a black Labrador who was born on October 17, 2014 and is now six-years-old.

Ever since I was little, I always had an interest in getting a guide dog. However, for a while, I expected to get my first guide dog after college. I thought after college would be a great time to get a dog, because I would be more confident, and I would know where I would be working. I maintained that belief throughout high school. Once I navigated through my freshman year of college, I began to change my mind and started thinking about applying during that year. I filled out an application for a guide dog in February 2016, and I went to training beginning on June 5, 2016, after the end of the school year. It has been one of the best decisions I have ever made. In a leap of faith, I had no idea what to expect out of the two-week training program. I am very grateful that I did.

There are a few reasons why I love having my guide dog. First, my guide dog's work is fantastic while also being a great companion. She is so much fun. She has a great personality, and she loves to play just like any dog. Her favorite activities when not doing guide work include chewing on Nyla bones, playing many games of tug of war, and running outside when given the opportunity while I am home for holidays or the summer. She is the sweetest dog, and we genuinely have a tremendous human-canine bond that continues to grow stronger each passing day.

Next, her guide work is impressive. Compared to traveling with a cane, I do not have to think as much. Yes, I have to know where I am going to give her directions, but I do not need to pay attention to every crack or dip in the sidewalk. I now have the assurance that when I tell her to go right, go to the curb, or go to the stairs, she will do it.

Navigating a college campus can be exhausting, but not having to think about every detail every second of every day consistently helps tremendously. Also, I noticed that I get to places and walk a lot quicker with my dog than with a cane. It is great. I can enjoy feeling the breeze and hearing the birds chirp while walking to class. My dog guides me around obstacles, stops for elevation changes, and pays attention to the environment around us.

I couldn't concentrate on these things as much when I was a cane user. Moreover, I feel I am more independent and feel more confident. I think she helps me to be more comfortable in many situations. I have found that more people are interested in learning about guide dogs. I have been able to meet even more people ever since she has been on Belmont's campus. We are a great team, and it has been a fantastic time. I cannot wait for even more adventures to come with her by my side.

It is worth getting a guide dog, and so is inheriting the responsibility that comes with taking care of a dog on your own. It is a big adjustment, but after a few weeks, you begin to establish a routine that works for both you and your dog. I would not change it for the world. My dog is such a great guide dog, and also a wonderful companion to navigate life with me. I am so fortunate I had the opportunity to attend the two-week training program in Oregon because it changed how I navigate my life for the better.

CHAPTER 7

MISADVENTURES OF MARNA AND ME

Aziza Rodriquez

My name is Aziza Rodriguez, and I have a female yellow Labrador named Marna. I am originally from Southern California, but I now reside in Denver, Colorado. I work as a Personal Care Attendant, and a Respite Care Provider, giving assistance and support to others with disabilities of various ages and backgrounds. I am a Girl Scouts of America volunteer and am serving a term with the Denver Mayor's Youth Commission. My passion lies with uplifting individuals with disabilities to reach their fullest potential, with a particular emphasis on children and the villages that raise them.

Adults around me made getting a guide dog sound inevitable, like a rite of passage, and my child self wasn't opposed to the idea of a constant companion. As I developed relationships with people I still call role models, I began to understand and envy the bond I witnessed between handler and dog. Having never been entirely confident using a cane, despite positive feedback from mobility instructors, I wanted the confidence and trust I observed in partnerships. Guide Dogs for the Blind (GDB) offered me the opportunity to reach that potential, to experience that bond, and learn so much from so many people. The soul-deep friendships that have developed because of my connection to GDB, and Marna, my first guide dog, are nothing short of magical.

My first indication that this lifestyle came with consequences I'd never considered was the first night I spent impatiently waiting for the veterinarian to open. Marna, diagnosed with Giardia, a parasite which attaches itself to the intestinal wall, resulting in an extremely upset tummy. We hadn't even lasted two weeks without disaster striking, and I was sure she would be removed from me by GDB. Contrary to my panicked thoughts, my local veterinary clinic, which offered all routine animal care and vaccinations free of charge. He offered discounted medications and irregular treatments and guided me through the recovery process expertly.

After conquering Giardia, Marna began to shed the angelic persona I had met in training and test me relentlessly. Every walk left me feeling like my arm was being ripped off due to dog distractions. Strangers were quick to provide judgmental commentary, and the frustrations of my family only added to the overall stressfulness of the situation. I remember sitting at home, petting her soft coat, which has a hint of volume to it, making her extra fluffy and soft, wondering if I had made a mistake. I doubted whether continuing to try was fair to her. With the excellent support of my field representative, I was able to understand how to issue effective corrections, and how to counterbalance the momentum of an excited lunging bundle of energy. With every successful route completed, we grew closer, and the trust between us blossomed.

Despite the tribulations we've faced together, I wholeheartedly believe Marna and I were made for each other. She is more than just a mobility tool; she is the embodiment of pure love. As a survivor of *retinoblastoma*, cancer that originates in the lining of the retinas, I understand the toll illness can have on a family. Cancer has touched the lives of so many loved ones beyond my own experience. When I learned that Marna had been instrumental in emotionally supporting and motivating our puppy-raiser through the pain and uncertainty of one child's cancer diagnosis, and another child's military deployment, I knew I'd been matched with an extraordinary dog.

Even though we now know our strengths and weaknesses, there are still off days. Days she refuses to drink water, days she insists on running me into snow-laden pine trees, days when leaping up to plant her paws on a pet shop window to gaze adoringly at the puppy on the other side seems appropriate. Some days feel like a prolonged correction when migraines and stress leave me incapable of giving commands that don't confuse her. However, there are also fantastic, flawless days where she finds our home when I've made a wrong turn or avoids a collapsed manhole cover. We're a team, through every good and bad day. Together, we face an annual analysis of her kidney functions and urinary incontinence and the subsequent heart in my throat discussions. Despite experiencing discrimination or harassment; together, we take each day in stride. She is my guide and confidant. I am devoted to her well-being. She holds my heart between her forepaws.

Out of harness, Marna is as sweet and mellow or wild and carefree as she wants to be on any given day. She can happily spend the day trying to get snuggles out of her favorite people or rampaging around the house with an obnoxious squeak toy. Marna loves rolling on her back, kicking her paws and snorting…very loudly. She adjusts to schedule inconsistencies with ease, and never backs down from a challenge or adventure. She's been known to ferret out snacks, both dog and human, no matter where they've been hiding. Overall, she is nothing more than a lover. If she is getting positive attention, her entire body vibrates with excitement. When positive attention is not forthcoming, she will harness the power of the sad puppy dog look until this problem is remedied.

What Marna has given me cannot be measured or put accurately into words. I could navigate the world without a guide, but with her, I am more confident while traveling. I've moved out of state, and into two apartments in entirely different areas of the city with her. I've been to concerts and amusement parks, on planes, trains, and even a few boats. I no longer feel anxiety about getting caught up in a swarming crush of bodies. We've participated in large scale protests to stand up for the civil rights that speak to me. With her, the disorientation of snow, wind, rain, or extreme levels of noise are easily pushed aside as we read each other's body language to get to where we need to be safely. Having a service dog may seem superfluous, but to those of us who choose this lifestyle, it can make the difference between living life to the fullest, and just living life.

The decision to retire is made by measuring her willingness and ability against her medical condition to work, compared to what changes I am willing to accommodate. My biggest fear was that important indicators would be masked by her boundless love and eagerness to please. She revels in praise and attention, requiring few leash corrections, and I worried that her spirit would want to continue longer than what would be best. With mixed emotions, I have definitively decided that Marna will not work past her eleventh birthday. There is a small measure of relief that I have a plan in place that will allow Marna to enjoy her old age in comfort. The day we hang up her harness will break both our hearts, even though she will have more than earned it. My gratitude towards those who have made this partnership possible. Since the gratitude only surpasses day one I feel for the dog who has taught me what it means to be a service dog handler, one paw print at a time.

Marna and I give thanks to the Smith family, our fantastic puppy-raisers, Cyndi Davis, our Guide Dogs for the Blind instructor, all of our field representatives, and the entire Guide Dogs for the Blind family. We wouldn't have made it without you. A special thanks to the most prominent service dog handling role models I had as a teen, Gail Paulson and Beth Mogarr for showing me what working and loving a dog looks like in real-time.

CHAPTER 8

PARTNERSHIP AT ITS BEST

Pat Pound

I decided to get a guide dog after thirty-five years as a cane traveler because I envied blind friends with dogs who traveled with ease in large open spaces and through crowds. I wanted a school that bred their own dogs, thinking that increased medical information could mean a longer life for the dog. I also wanted an area of the country that had weather and a lifestyle similar to my own. I got my first guide from Guide Dogs for the Blind (GDB) in 2003. I truly loved the experience, especially the partnership.

I found that meeting her needs, feeding, relieving, and loving her was a welcome break during the day, instead of a burden. We traveled a lot, and it was sometimes frustrating when we couldn't find a suitable relief area or trash can. For the most part, it was great fun and very beneficial to have a guide in an isolated area. Germaine, my first guide, worked 11½ years, which was well over our school's average. My second guide, Iris, is equally accomplished and totally dedicated to her work.

I particularly enjoy GDB's approach to allowing you to interact with your dog's puppy-raisers. With both dogs, this has been a rewarding experience. I also love that GDB is using food rewards. I have experienced both leash correction and food reward training, and I definitely prefer the latter. I benefited from their veterinary assistance program, which helped me through a couple of expensive surgeries and illnesses.

I find that people interact with me more readily as a dog handler than as a cane user. When I travel, I meet people who miss their dogs and want to talk. I sometimes can get information during the conversation that helps me improve my orientation without them even knowing it. People do get on my nerves sometimes, especially when they push to pet my dog. I use a sign written as "Please Do Not Feed or Flirt with Me" and it seems to work well. People laugh when they read it, and it breaks the spell of intent to pet.

I have not encountered many difficulties in access to public places like stores and restaurants. Whenever questioned, I have been able to supply sufficient information to solve the problem. Sometimes there is confusion if businesses try to apply rules about pet dogs to service dogs. Again, education is the key. Sometimes simple solutions exist. For example, at my workplace, I put a plastic floor protector underneath my dog's bed. It helps the cleaning people with loose dog hair. Similarly, at the gym, I use a small yoga mat to cut down on dog hair and also keep my dog dry at the pool. I choose to frequent restaurants that have enough space between tables that my dog is not at risk of getting stepped on.

Both my dogs are the most loyal and patient creatures. All they really want is to serve me and do well. My personal goal: take care of each of my dogs as well as they take care of me. That means understanding the personality of each dog and devoting the time and energy to meet their needs. I believe that the higher our standards for ourselves as dog handlers are, the more accepting others will be of our dogs.

As I am now retired, I try to vary my dog's experiences. We go to different places frequently, and I introduce new games or routes to keep Iris happy and focused. My goal moving forward is to give her as much love and concern as she gives me.

To my first guide dog, Germaine, who will always be top dog!

PART 3

LIFE ADJUSTMENTS

CHAPTER 9

LEARNING FROM NOLAN

Frank Lopez

After having used a white cane for more than twenty years, I was diagnosed with a hearing loss. My doctor recommended that I look into getting a guide dog. I spent some time researching some guide dog organizations. I chose Guide Dogs for the Blind (GDB) in San Raphael, California. I can remember an intake worker asking me what type of dog and what type of temperament of dog I was interested. I replied, "I want one that I can trust my life to, a very social dog that would fit well with my high school teaching environment, and one that is smarter than me!" Their immediate response was, "That will be easy!" I received Nolan, my yellow Labrador guide dog, in 2010 and we have been joined at the hip ever since.

Nolan is genuinely a social animal. He loves to interact with people, especially ladies and children. I think it has something to do with their high-pitched voices. I like to tease that Nolan should have been named "Casanolan." He loves to do his job, and he seems to take great pride in it. I am continually learning what Nolan is capable of doing. When I first got Nolan, my wife, Judy and I would go grocery shopping together with Nolan at my side. She would read off our grocery list as we go down the aisles and unbeknownst to me, Nolan was a soaking in all of the information. One day, I asked Nolan to take me to the milk, and he did. I WAS dumbfounded! He loves to find things for me in the grocery store and can guide me to more than one hundred food items by name. I am always surprised at what he knows, and I sometimes see if he knows a product that I rarely get. Of course, a kibble reward will help to reinforce his memory. People often stop and stare and ask me if I am training Nolan. My typical reply is, "He is training me!"

What makes Nolan genuinely unique and special is his ability to empathize with people. I noticed this early on when I was teaching. When Nolan came in contact with a special needs student or a physically disabled one, he would seem to sense that they needed his attention. He would go up to strangers in a wheelchair or using a walker and want to comfort them.

In December of 2012, we moved to Sun Prairie, Wisconsin, and we have acclimated ourselves to the community. Everyone seems to remember Nolan's name and not mine, but he is a real ice breaker. He helps me to overcome social barriers. On the advice of my sister-in-law, Nolan and I went up to visit the nearby senior center when we first moved. While we were there, Nolan went up to an elderly lady in her wheelchair, and she immediately asked if she could pet him. That gave me the idea of visiting the seniors once a week, and they really enjoy Nolan's visits. Most of them look forward to our visits except for a few who are suffering from dementia. For them, it is a whole new experience each visit. It's kind of cute when a senior would exclaim, "And, who is this dog? What's his name?" Her friend would then say, "Oh, Margaret, this is Nolan. He comes all of the time!" Many seniors then start telling me stories of the dogs they used to have, and memories would begin flooding forward. Sometimes, they would cry remembering their pets from the past. At this point, they would hug Nolan all the more as he sits patiently near them.

My son, Andrew, volunteered at the senior center in their computer lab. He also helped out serving meals and cleaned up afterward. My wife, Judy, spends a portion of her time driving me back and forth so that we can meet our volunteer commitments. We have gotten to be relatively well known and are very much appreciated. Nolan, Andrew, Judy, and I were honored as Volunteer Family of the Year at a United Way luncheon. Nolan has taught me that you should never stop learning or contributing because you always will receive more than you give.

I wish to dedicate my story to puppy-raisers who unselfishly give of their time and love.

CHAPTER 10

MY BLACK BEAUTY

Carolyn Dale Newell

Navigating the world with a white cane limited me. I felt uncomfortable depending on it, not because I did not want to use it, but the white cane did not earn my trust. Whenever a sighted guide was available, I preferred it over the white cane since it cannot compete with another set of eyes. I felt my safety was in jeopardy, and I wanted a guide dog for extra security.

I chose Guiding Eyes for the Blind (GEB) in Yorktown Heights, New York, because a friend highly recommended this school. She was pleased with her dog from GEB. I only looked into one other school when I feared my home interview did not go well. I learned that many applicants feel their phone or home interview doesn't go well. Perhaps it is from nerves. The day I was accepted was joyful, and a few months later, I got the call with a class date.

During the time I waited for my class date to arrive, I got in shape by walking three miles daily, and my alarm set at 6 a.m. I doubt we ever walked three miles at school, but it kept this 54-year-old from tiring out as quickly. I thought I would be the oldest student, but our class ranged from ages 30 to 74.

Guiding Eyes matched me with a healthy two-year-old black Labrador, Iva, to meet my needs. I truly enjoyed my three weeks of training at GEB. They covered all my expenses: airfare, meals, training, equipment, and Iva. The instructors encouraged us as we trained. They knew just how to help us as visually impaired students. They prepared scrumptious meals, provided housekeeping, and gave us a safe atmosphere with their nursing staff.

Everyone arrived on Monday and Tuesday was the day we met our potential friend. On our initial walk, I felt an enormous sense of freedom. For the first time, I could walk at a quick pace without fear of running into someone or something. I had a set of eyes watching out for me, giving me more confidence at noisy intersections. I was no longer afraid to walk in new places. The door to independence opened through Guiding Eyes and Iva.

GEB supports graduates financially with several funds. They will reimburse me for any veterinarian expenses up to $300 annually, provided I am current with required check-ups and sending health records to GEB, and Iva maintains her weight. An emergency fund is also available if needed. Trainers answer questions, and someone will even come out to work the more difficult issues out with you. I will apply for transfer of title two years after our graduation, and Iva will legally become my dog. GEB's support is available for Iva's lifetime, and the transfer of title does not affect that. When Iva's working days are over, I will return to GEB for my next dog.

Iva and I are doing things I have not independently done in twenty years. I have never enjoyed independence on vacations, but now we can leave the hotel and venture out without my husband. Guide dogs are not limited to helping us get from point A to point B. They can take you to your chair, table, door, or mailbox. GEB teaches you how to train them to target objects. Iva even helps me retrieve things I drop on the floor. She is extremely loving and cares about what is happening to me. Iva's puppy-raiser did a great job, and we have an excellent relationship. That is all based on an individual's preferences, but I have found it helpful.

The only drawback we have encountered is irresponsible dog owners. People don't obey leash laws, allowing their pets to interfere with us. Some people bring aggressive dogs in public, and they bark and growl at Iva. I knew to expect some of that, but I did not realize it would be a reoccurring problem.

I have had dogs before, but the relationship between a guide and its handler is unique. It is as deep as the bond between a child and parent or even a husband and wife. I am overwhelmed with the joy my guide dog brings me. She is not just a guide; she is my best friend.

I wish to dedicate this chapter to my black beauty, Iva.

CHAPTER 11

SIDE BY SIDE PARTNERSHIP

Dave Steele

It has been just over a year since my guide dog, Christopher, came into our lives. Although I'm not there yet, the difference he made has been incredible. Three years ago, my world came crashing down after my diagnosis with *retinitis pigmentosa* (RP), a hereditary eye condition with no treatment or cure. My vision began to decline rapidly, starting with the loss of my peripheral vision. Viewing the world through an ever-shrinking tunnel can be pretty scary. RP didn't just rob me of my sight, but also my confidence and independence. I felt anxious just to step outside my front door, and I was afraid to travel anywhere on my own.

In a bid to win back my independence, I applied for a guide dog a few months after my diagnosis. I was determined to take the help out there to win back my pride and independence. I was made aware from the beginning by the charity, Guide Dogs UK, that it could be as long as two years to be matched with a suitable dog. However, after speaking to other guide dog owners, I knew that it would be worth the wait.

After 18 months, I got the phone call that would change everything. It is a day I will never forget. My wife Amy and I were on our way out to lunch to celebrate the release of my first poetry book, *Stand by Me RP*, when my mobility instructor called to say that they had found Christopher, a potential match for me. The instructor asked if I would like to meet him in a couple of days. Amy broke down in tears, while a mixture of emotions ran through my head all at once. We met Christopher for the first time. I got to walk a couple of blocks with him in his harness to see if I was a match for his pace.

A couple of days later, I was leaving home for a ten-day residential course to train with Christopher. I remember feeling sick the night before, and anxious with the million questions that were swirling through my mind. Was I ready? Would I be able to handle a guide dog? Would he fit into our lives? The next few weeks were a total blur. I knew that once I had Christopher, I wouldn't be able to hide my vision loss anymore. I would have that label in public. I threw myself into the training, and the partnership with Christopher immediately began to blossom. With each day, I felt my anxiety lessen and regain my confidence little by little. I learned how much of a partnership it is when having a guide dog. I put my trust in him to work together as a team. A couple of weeks later, we were qualified, and my official training was over.

However, my real-world training continues to this day. Without an instructor by our side, it is just Christopher and me. Each day, we face new challenges. Due to people's misconceptions and lack of awareness about guide dogs, I often have people assuming I'm training him rather than him being my guide dog. People sometimes commented that I don't look like a blind person. I have had people and other animals distracting Christopher while he's working, which can cause problems. It throws us off our stride, takes his attention away from the task at hand, and in doing so, puts me in danger. We have to avoid obstacles daily such as cars parked on the sidewalks, which is a real problem here in the United Kingdom.

Like any relationship, we both have our off days. Christopher isn't a machine and can be a right stroppy on some days, especially if we walk past a park on our way to somewhere. However, like any good partnership, we support each other. I know that things take time, yet, it is so worthwhile. Christopher has given me back my independence. The ability to pop out to the shops without having to rely on Amy is something I will never take for granted again.

I dedicate my chapter to Christopher for helping me find myself again. Amy, my children, and I will forever be thankful to have Christopher in our lives.

CHAPTER 12

NIGHT AND DAY

Jackie Hollenbeck

On February 8, 2004, I was medically diagnosed with *retinitis pigmentosa* (RP), a breakdown and loss of red cells in the retina, which can lead to varying degrees of vision loss over some time. Today, I have five degrees of vision remaining. Life was looking good for me as a Master Nail Technician until my ophthalmologist told me I would have to give up driving. After leaving the ophthalmologist's office, I pulled over to cry. I called my mom, but we were both so confused with the diagnosis, so she asked many questions that I didn't have the answers to give her.

After lengthy research about *retinitis pigmentosa*, my mom suggested I get a guide dog. She made calls to inquire about guide dogs and found a school that did not require mobility training. The school sent me an application to fill out, and I was accepted a week later.

I attended my first school for all but nine days of the training month and ended up leaving without a dog named Sadi, a Doberman. The school was unprepared to handle my probing questions about the dogs matching to its students. My concerns increased that Sadi showed aggression towards the other dogs in my class. The extreme measures used to discipline and control the dog had me concerned as well, so I asked more questions. Uncomfortable with the lack of information the school was providing regarding my concerns, I decided to leave the program.

After leaving the school disappointed, I went on to obtain a new dog, Hershey, from a reputable breeder, a handsome male Doberman. He had the help of police trainers and Texas DARS Orientation and Mobility Instructor to train him how to be a guide dog and a hearing dog. Sadly, Hershey passed away on October 14, 2017, and I was blessed to have him in my life for 12 years and ten days.

I learned about Leader Dogs for the Blind in Rochester Hills, Michigan, through a friend who had recently obtained her guide from them. After learning about her experience, I wanted to know more about the school, and I looked into their deafblind courses; I had been re-diagnosed with *Usher syndrome* Type 2. *Usher syndrome* typically results in partial or total hearing and vision loss that can worsen over time. After this newest diagnosis, I received cochlear implants to help with my hearing loss.

While researching the Leader Dog's program and courses, I discovered that it isn't necessary to know American Sign Language (ASL) to enter into the program. Leader Dog's classes run twice a year, in May and in August. Each class consists of two instructors and four students. The amount of time spent training was described as steady and consistent. The only downtime is when other students are working with trainers, and one must wait their turn. Individual attention and consideration of every detail were things that Leader Dogs for the Blind prided itself on.

My new dog, Willow, a Golden Retriever-Labrador cross, was 18-months-old at the time I attended class. She is beautiful and full of personality. We trained together for nineteen days and had a blast! The weather in Michigan during that May posed difficulties. It snowed the first day, and the next day it was 85 degrees and humid. I participated in all the exercises, except once when I could not walk the outdoors trail. I had to make sure Willow did not overheat. My instructor was very understanding and allowed us to go back to the bus to cool off.

Everything else about the school was excellent. The food was spectacular in a restaurant setting style; it's possible to request special meals, no matter the reason. The volunteers are always there to assist students. Students are allowed to spend free time on or off-campus. I have kept in touch with one of my classmates since graduation.

After graduating, Willow and I boarded the plane home and sat next to a lovely lady. It was my first exposure to the real world as a guide dog owner, and it was awesome. Willow slept the whole time. She never had to relieve herself. She was a perfect angel for the entire seven-hour flight back to Texas. We made it through security and back home to greet Hershey, my retired guide dog, and introduce them to each other for the first time. We chose a neutral ground at the park for them to meet. It went off beautifully!

Service dogs are a big responsibility; to consider expected adjustments. I had to remember to incorporate Willow when going through the doorways in my house. At first, there were a lot of accidents because Hershey was confused at first to why he was no longer accompanying me. He would get so excited when I pulled Willow's harness out but got upset when Willow and I left. It's very common for many retired dogs to feel emotional as being replaced. I would praise and love on Hershey for his new role in his retirement before I leave my home with Willow.

After being home from Leader Dogs for a month, I was ready for my next adventure. I was going to live at a residential training facility for the blind during the next four months. I was prepared to learn more independent living skills while bonding with my dog, Willow. We had a busy class schedule but had weekends to ourselves. The school, a city well-adapted to deafblind individuals, is located in Austin, Texas. Not long after we arrived, we met another guide dog team. Willow was in love with this dog, and I planned many playdates. Unfortunately, Willow became quite lazy, so I contacted Leader Dogs for their assistance, and they counseled me. Other issues I had with Willow was her begging for food and her disinterest in working. Leader Dogs was able to help me manage Willow's begging and offer helpful steps to keep her focused and motivated in her work. I appreciated that Leader Dogs was there for me every step of the way. After four months, we graduated from the residential training facility, and Willow and I went home.

The first year after graduating from Leader Dogs on June 3, 2016, brought a lot of drama, excitement, heartbreak, and love. It also marked the time that Willow became mine forever after the transferred ownership. Leader Dogs helped to offset the cost of healthcare expenses for Willow by sending me a check for her first veterinary check-up. I was able to find a great veterinarian and establish a relationship with her. Willow also gets her allotted monthly heart-worm, flea, and tick medications since we have a lot of these critters here in Texas. A few days before leaving the program, Leader Dogs provided all graduating students with the first six months of maintenance medications, a three-year rabies vaccination, and up-to-date medical records. The dogs, microchipped under the school's name, allow the handlers to add their information to it after a year.

I have realized that not only is Willow my eyes when out in public, but she's also my closest companion dog. She matches my pace perfectly and is very alert to me, my needs, and my surroundings. Willow follows me everywhere. Whenever I take a step, she is always there. She is an earnest worker, bless her heart, and she's very serious about playtime. Playtime is almost like watching a kid opening Christmas presents. She is also very serious about her food and treats. She insists on both, and they better be on time.

Willow and I have been an excellent team for three years, and when she turns ten-years-old, I will retire her and keep her. I hope to try Leader Dog's program again in the future. They have a pilot program to train dogs as a guide dog and a hearing alert dog combined. In the meantime, I am excited to say that I am in the last stage of an application process to receive a hearing alert dog.

CHAPTER 13

WHAT A BEAUTIFUL DOG: MY FOUR PAW DRIVE

Shari Atchison

I am a massage therapist and a mom of two grown children. I like to walk and to read, and I love listening to 80's and country music. To me, life is what you make it. I strive to live, laugh often, recognize many things to be grateful for and to find simple things to enjoy.

I have *Usher syndrome*, a genetic disease that causes deaf-blindness. It is an autosomal recessive disease. Each parent passes the *Usher syndrome* gene to the child, and the child is born with some degree of hearing loss paired with gradual vision loss. In some instances, the child is born with normal hearing, then progressively lose some or all of it later in life. *Retinitis pigmentosa* (RP), a group of degenerative retinal eye diseases, is the cause of my vision loss. A person with *Usher syndrome* will show signs of night blindness, continuously restricted peripheral vision (tunnel vision) and depth perception, color, and light adaption. One's vision might degenerate by getting worse, stabilizing for a while, and then get worse again. Everyone progresses with RP at different rates. Some go blind quickly, some in their 50s, and there are some with residual vision well into their 70s.

I dealt with a lot of denials related to my *Usher syndrome*. I wore hearing aids all my life, and I was bussed to another city to be in class with other deaf kids. I learned American Sign Language (ASL) and used it at school, but when I went home every night, I spoke. No one signed. I never thought anything of it. It was just the way it was. I had an older brother and sister with hearing loss, though their loss was not as bad as mine.

I was 29 years old when I finally was handed with the news. The ophthalmologist solemnly told me one December day he was confident I had RP. He asked if I was driving. He stated it is dark outside because he knew night vision is terrible for people with RP. I managed to drive home that night, but in tears. I guess I knew all along in the back of my mind. My two older siblings with hearing loss were also diagnosed with RP a few years earlier. I always wondered if there was a link between their hearing loss and RP.

Regardless, I carried on. I pushed it away from my thoughts. I could still see, and I was still functioning as "normal." I had a toddler to raise. Life went on. I went through a divorce and got remarried and had another child. I learned how to use the computer and looked up more information on *Usher syndrome*. By that time, we knew that the hearing loss and RP were linked. I found a couple of e-mail message lists and found courage and understanding by those who also had *Usher syndrome*. I was not alone. They offered great resources and had "been there" or experienced what I was going through in many ways.

After I gave up driving, I learned that a person doesn't pick up the white cane and use it. The visually impaired or blind person learns the safest ways to travel to remain mobile and independent. It is called Orientation and Mobility (O&M). The O&M instructor shows you how to sweep the cane in front of you, like a third leg. It can tactilely alert the cane user to obstacles and drop offs, such as curbs and descending stairways. The instructor also teaches traffic assessment at all intersections from street light to four-way stop signs.

I shortly learned that once a cane user obtains an O&M skill, they can apply to get a guide dog. The visually impaired person or blind person cannot get a guide dog without the O&M

training because they need to know how to travel safely with a dog effectively. They also will need to use the cane as a backup when the guide dog is sick, has to stay at the veterinary clinic for surgery or injury, or other unexpected situations.

Now, I have a new journey. I have done the cochlear implant (CI) journey, the white cane journey, and now, I have the guide dog journey. Life is a never-ending journey, full of adjustments and change.

It was finally here. It was "Dog Day" at Guide Dog Foundation (GDF) in Smithtown, New York, on Long Island. Dog Day is the day they give you the dog who is going to be your partner and keep you safe and guide you. The trainer just gave me the leash to this happy, black Labrador puppy. The dog just popped into the room and I was to sit and hold its leash.

When I first laid eyes on this black bundle of energy, I had no idea what hard work it would be. I've spoken to numbers of guide dog handlers who have had guide dogs, and they raved about how much their dogs helped them, from finding a seat to getting across a street safely. I thought it was going to be a piece of cake. I grew up with dogs and loved them.

At GDF, there were two groups of students. There was a group of first-time users getting their first-ever guide dogs. The second group was a retrains who were getting their second or successor dogs. Both groups were all informed the night before Dog Day what their dogs' names, breed, and gender were. My instructor told me I was getting a female black Labrador named "Nyla." I went over the name, Nyla. It took me another day to realize it was not Nyla. It was "Nala." I just misheard it.

I watched this new dog who has just had a bath start rolling on the floor and chase her tail. I have never seen a dog chase her tail so fast, spinning for as long as she did. She looked at me, sniffed me, then went to the door when she heard the trainer's voice in the hall and started whining. I called her to me, to let her know everything was okay. The poor girl was already missing the trainer. When the trainer returned to check on us, he said, "Look at the hair on the floor!" I told him that Nala was rolling on the floor. I later learned that she would blow her coat all over the place after a bath. I needed to keep her brushed.

Afterward, she and I found out how much effort it took to work together. She already knew her stuff, but she had to adjust to me, not the trainer. I am a soft-spoken person. I learned I had to speak to her loud enough to direct her to what I wanted her to do. I learned many commands: Left, right, straight, to the curb, halt, over left, over right, follow, forward, and a few others. We also had to always praise our dogs for doing the work we wanted them to do by saying, "Good dog!", "Awesome!" and "Wonderful!" If I am sitting on a chair, and if there are no obstacles, she will sit under my chair. I use the words "down and under" command. Otherwise, I would command her to sit in the front or beside me.

We spent the next three weeks learning to walk together on the sidewalks, streets, in the mall, through revolving doors, walking along the side of train station' platform, doing country walks, and we also practiced going through the airport security check. We have had two-night walks. With RP, I am night-blind. I rarely go far alone in the dark, unless I have some light I can see. I had to work on feeling my dog's movements and have her guide me around obstacles on the sidewalks. It was extremely tough to "let go" and let her do the work. There are times when I do get disoriented, and I need to get my bearings or have to ask directions. The dog does not have a built-in GPS. The dog may know repetitious routes, but as a responsible handler I need to know where I am at all times so I can command my dog to do her job effectively. We also had a traffic check. Often, a trainer in disguise would drive a vehicle to purposely cut us off in the street or the driveway. Nala did great in her job when she stopped and prevented me from being in harm's way.

We learned about obedience training, which I do every day with Nala. I have her sit and do a down-stay. It is a simple task. The dog has to sit, lay down, and then stay down. I would walk around her, and she has to remain in the down-stay position. Once I completed my trip around her, I would tell her, "Up-sit" and she would get up and sit upright. Through praise and kibbles, she does excellent work. It teaches the dog to stay down when we want them to. My dog has to remain in the down position so, people can move about her. I might change it up and dance around her or walk across her body like I am stepping over her. Sometimes, I walk away from her and drop a book behind her. I want to make sure she stays, and she does. She is rewarded with praise and kibbles.

About a year ago, my instructor was showing the class where a particular muscle located on the skeleton; it was hanging on the stand; it slipped off and crashed to the floor, about a foot from Nala's nose. Nala did not jump, get up, or freak out. She remained under my chair as I was sitting at the front row. It all happened so fast that it took me a few seconds to realize what had happened. I was very pleased that Nala did not get spooked.

These dogs are trained in "intelligent disobedience" and will disobey a command if it is not safe. Nala has done this a couple of times since we became a team. I would listen for traffic, and when I was ready, I would say to her, "Forward" and she would take me across the street. I would wait for her to make the first move. I could not just walk and have her follow because she had to lead me. If she did not move forward, I could not move. She is disobeying my command because it is not safe to cross.

One time, I was at a street corner I wanted to cross. I listened and heard no cars. I said, "Forward!" and Nala did not move. I was puzzled because I was sure I did not hear anything, and suddenly I felt the wind, and something just whizzed by in front of me. We could have been seconds away from a run-in with a bicycle. "Good girl, Nala!" And, we continued our routine.

These dogs have to pass required tests to be a guide dog. They cannot spook easily. If a dog gets scared about something and that interferes with their guide work or welfare, the dog will not likely pass the graduation testing. If the dog is already working with a handler, then the dog may be forced into early retirement. Retirement for a guide dog is merely that, where the dog becomes a pet. Most dogs retire because of old age and/or health issues.

We also learned how to handle distractions. Guide dogs may be working dogs, but they are still dogs. A correction will get the dog's attention and redirect their attention to concentrating on their handler and not the distraction. A quick snapping tug to the leash or harness and the dog is back on the job, guiding the handler. The distractions I deal with the most are other dogs and small children.

Nala likes to greet other passing dogs, she will tug, she will drag, or she will whip around. It is my job to give the handle of the harness a quick backward push and say, "No, leave it!! Straight!" This command brings her attention back to me and her job, and we continue walking. Sometimes I would have to do this several times, and she knew I don't want her meeting the other dog because we needed to keep walking. Corrections like these do not punish the dog. It is like a tap on the shoulder "Pay attention!"

When we come across a small child, Nala will want to go to that child. She is a "big dog" to that child. I will hold her back with a quick, "Leave it!" As we walk along the sidewalk, Nala will want to sniff the grass, and I will have to correct her and say, "No, leave it!"

When I was still training with Nala at the guide dog school, there was a fenced-in area where we were able to let the dogs run. We each had a bag of kibbles. We were to call our dogs to us with kibbles in our hands. The first time we did this, Nala and another dog went to the wrong person. We had to give the dogs another handful of kibbles. Then, we were to let them run and play again.

"Go play!" We called their names once again, and they came running to us and the kibbles. We praised them and let them play again. It is essential to know that they always come to us when called, even if we do not have some kibbles with us. If the dog got loose and running outside, maybe into the street, we would be saving the dog's life by calling them to come to us. The dog would hear us say, "Come!" The dog may have been in a potentially dangerous position, and we got their attention to come back to us.

Nala does not go far when she knows I have kibbles; she wants those kibbles. The way to her heart is her stomach. I don't worry too much if she's loose because I know she will come to me when called. She wants her food!

There are many great things I love about Nala, but there is one story in particular. We had gotten a lot of groceries, and the screen door was wide open. Nala would only look out the door but would not cross the threshold. She'd stay inside. I found out later it was not what she was trained to do at the school. It was just something "extra" that the puppy-raiser did because she had other dogs and was concerned for their safety if they should run out the open door.

Puppy-raisers are exceptionally dedicated people who raise the dog as a puppy. They housebreak them; they socialize them in all sorts of situations, and use of transportation such as planes, buses, trains, and cars. A puppy-raiser may have other pets, young or adult children, or may live alone in a busy city, a quiet suburb, or the countryside. I am thankful for all the puppy-raisers who give their time to take care of a puppy for a year or more, love the puppy, and know they will have to return the dog to the school for service dog training.

Going about life at home with Nala is not always perfect. Another command we use is "find." Find the seat. Find the door. One day a couple of months after we got home from school, I got on a bus. I told her to "find the seat!" She led me right to a person sitting on one of the seats. The lady laughed. Nala was wagging her tail, sniffing her. The lady says, "She smells my cat." The lady's laugh was positive reinforcement for Nala. I quickly told Nala, "Good girl, not that seat. Find another seat. An empty one." A seat is a seat. Many people think it's so cute and they will laugh, so I have to correct Nala. Just ignore the dog and let them do the work.

We go to the store. "Find the door!". Nala leads me to the door. It is not the automatic doors I am looking for, but to her, it is a door. She did her job. I have to praise her for that and "find another door." A door is a door. She did find the exit door.

One day, I was walking around the neighborhood. I saw a little girl run ahead of her mother, excitedly. She asked me if she could pet my dog. I told her no and explained that my dog was working. I felt so bad, and the mom just gave me the meanest glare. I just said, "She's a working dog. I'm sorry. I need her to stay focused on her job." I admit that if I were not in a hurry to go somewhere, I'd take her harness off to let her pet Nala. I do break the rules sometimes, but it is rare.

The first year I had Nala, we did a lot of learning together, especially me. Nala knows her stuff, but as a kid, she'll see what she can get away without my knowledge. Within the first month, after I took her home from school, I took Nala around the neighborhood. She would slow down, and I realized there were a lot of "helicopter" seeds that fall from the maple tree. We had an early spring that year, and they were already falling and scattered all over the sidewalks. Nala was eating them. I quickly grabbed a couple of helicopters and put them on the driveway. I would walk her back and forth, passing the helicopter seeds so I could work on her about not touching them. She made a wide "I'm not going near it" path. She knew I was not going to allow her to try to eat it.

I would practice this with crackers or bread. I would throw it on the sidewalk or driveway, and we would pass it. Nala knows

I'm aware of its presence. She will try to pull one on me if we are in a restaurant and there is food on the floor. Nala would fast head dive for the food item. It happens so fast, and I am ready to say, "No, leave it!"

About 75% of the time, when Nala and I are out and about, I would hear someone exclaim, "What a beautiful dog!" "You have a beautiful dog!" I had one say, "I am not a dog person, but that is one beautiful dog!" People approach me in many different ways. Some want to pet her so bad, and I have to say, "I'm sorry, she's working." Sometimes, I would take her harness off and then I'd let them pet her, so she always associates having the harness off when petted. It probably only happens about 10% of the time.

Some people talk to me from 5 yards away, and I am not able to hear them well, and I fall back on the motions of guessing what they say and knowing it is mostly about her. "What kind of dog is she?" "She looks like my dog" "I have Lab(s) at home. They are great dogs!" Or, I would get, "He is a handsome dog...it is a boy, right?" And, sometimes, I would get, "Are you in training? Are you training her?" What? Me? "No, I am not training her. She's my dog. She's working for me." They will look at me and say "oh." Some expect you to be entirely blind to have a guide dog. Sometimes, store employees think I'm training her, too.

We continue to be a "work in progress." Some days are so routine we are fine, other times things break up our usual routine because we are in a new area or a building we have never been to before, and I need to orient myself to have her guide me by giving her the commands she is trained to do.

I was in a store I had never shopped. By the checkout, there was a whole wall of windows. It was bright. It was like weapons of mass confusion for me. Are any of these windows a door to get outside? I was a little apprehensive, but I tried to be confident when I picked up the bag and just said, "Find the door! Find the door outside!" And, I could feel some eyes on us as she marched me to an automated door that opened for us as we approached it. "Awesome, Nala!" She did it!

Another time, we were at the mall. I needed to use the women's bathroom. I went to the accessible stall because it was larger and would have more room for both of us. Nala stuck her nose under that stall's wall before I could tell her not to. Suddenly, I heard the woman in that stall scream. Oops! Who would expect to see a dog's nose sticking under the stall you are using? I was feeling so bad at the time, but looking back on it, it did have a humorous note to it.

When Nala and I went to church together, she would lie down quietly. Every time I had to get up, I'd have to let her know she had to stay. She got used to the times I kept getting up and getting back down during the church service. She learned if I got my purse, then it was time to go. During the sermon part, when we all sat for a while, you would start to hear snoring. Yep. She was sleeping and snoring in church, and she is not a quiet about it. For a girl, she snores with some snorts, even. I would have to give her a pat on the head to wake her up yet keep her lying down and not to get up. It was a church. Shhh.

She has also snored during class. It was a kind of a catch-22. She could get away with falling asleep in class. The teacher took a picture of her, catching her red-pawed, sleeping in class. She does work very hard sometimes. Downtime is still being on the clock.

Today, we have been together for about 7 years. Nala's going to be 9-years-old in the summer of 2019. She is a sweet and loving dog. Her tail is always ready to wag at a moment's notice. She never barks, and she loves attention. She says hi to the regular clients at the office. When she's snoring or dreaming during the sessions at work, I like to joke that she is a working dog and gets to sleep on the job.

At home, Nala would grab a toy and play with it and likes to play, especially when I have visitors over. Everyone loves Nala. What is there not to love about a sweet-natured dog. When I or someone else is showering, she lies down right by the bathroom door. You can feel a warm spot on the carpet right outside the door. It's probably her way of saying, "I got you."

She is a fantastic dog. Nala loves her praises for good work. She's a Labrador and Labradors love their food and snacks. I will put a cup (she gets two meals a day, one cup each. She will eat it in 30 seconds flat, her tail wagging as she eats. She has a dog bowl at work that a friend has given her. On the bottom of the bowl is a picture of a dog with the word "Happy" written over the dog's head. It describes her to a T. I always think about taking a video of her eating out of that bowl, tail wagging as she eats. Then, when she's done, zooming to the bowl to show the drawing of a dog with the word "Happy". Everyone loves Nala. What is there not to love about a sweet-natured dog?

We all have our stories, our journeys with each of our guide dogs. And our stories won't be the same with the next guide dog we have. The most important thing is to be safe and has a good working relationship together as a team.

I dedicate my chapter to Nala, my two daughters, puppy-raisers, all service dogs - past, present, and future, - and all who supported me on my journey.

PART 4

PERSEVERANCE AND MIRACLES

CHAPTER 14

SPUNKS AND SMARTS: BUCKLEY'S STORY

Annemarie Agers

In January of 2018, I was talking to a friend about my frustration obtaining a service dog for my husband. Danny was a 100% disabled veteran with *Post Traumatic Stress Disorder (PTSD), Traumatic Brain Injury* (TBI), and many physical issues. He had applied to many of the non-profit organizations only to be turned down. My friend connected me with Matt Burgess of Freedom Fidos. He was so eager to help us out, and Matt was willing to do the training.

On February 2018, we received Buckley. I remember the day at the Freedom Fidos Danny was asked to pick which puppy from a litter he wanted. Danny asked to be left alone in a room with the two puppies he picked so he could interact with each of them and make his decision. It didn't take long before he came out with Buckley in his arms.

He said, "I want this one. He's got spunk!" And, boy, does he, and he has lots of smarts as well! They formed a bond so quickly, and I could see the joy on my husband's face as he held his new dog. A pure joy that I had not seen in a long time. Fortunately, because we only live 20 minutes away, Danny was able to keep Buckley at home and take him to Freedom Fidos to prepare Buckley in becoming a service dog.

My husband struggled with many demons, but he was willing to put in the work to train a service dog. The handler needs as much training as the dog, if not more! Matt and Danny quickly formed an extraordinary and close friendship. Danny enjoyed meeting and spending time with Matt to train Buckley. He doesn't form friendships like this one so quickly, or often. I know that Matt was a blessing to him.

Now, I have to tell you something about myself. I am not a pet or an animal person. They are beautiful in someone else's homes. However, we already had a dog and a cat, both belonging to my son. Despite my feelings about animals, I was very much in favor of having Buckley, because a service dog would be a big help to my husband.

Throughout the years, I tolerated my son's two pets, but there was something about Buckley that made it so easy to love him. All of a sudden, I found myself letting a dog on my bed and even my couch. I was enjoying him because I was so happy to see the joy and the help Buckley brought to Danny.

Unfortunately, my husband could not seem to overcome many of his demons. He succumbed to them on June 4, 2018. In a short time, he and Buckley were a team; they grew so close. Buckley knew just when to put his head in Danny's lap or when he was able to do physical tasks that were difficult for Danny.

After Danny passed away, I asked Kristine and Matt to keep Buckley until I could make some decisions. They wholeheartedly agreed to keep Buckley, and they continued to work with and love him. They gave him special treatment as they helped him through the loss of Danny. I kept telling them that I just wasn't sure what I was going to do. Here I was, a non-pet person, and I already had sole responsibility for two pets. Let's face it; how much do the kids do for their pets? Could I keep a third pet in my home? Matt and Kristine were so patient and understanding while telling me they would keep him as long as I needed, and that Buckley was all mine unless I chose otherwise.

Eventually, Buckley would go back and forth between his two sets of parents! We co-parented that dog for quite a while, and it worked out so well. Finally, in early 2019, after Matt and

Kristine had kept Buckley for a little while, I asked them to bring him back home to me.

I knew in my heart that I was keeping him permanently. I couldn't verbalize it though. It was with mixed feelings that I finally made the right decision. Matt and Kristine had done so much for us, and I knew Matt could benefit from having a younger service dog as well. Buckley is a living connection to my husband. They always told me that it was okay if I decided to keep him. They brought him home for the final time.

I like to think Matt and Kristine could sense what was going through my head at this time. Something I do know is that the day I finally said, "I'm keeping him," they were so very happy for me. They joyfully told me they thought this was the right decision.

Buckley goes to work with me on most days. My bosses and co-workers are very accepting of him. There are days that my responsibilities at work make it difficult, and then he has to stay home. Fortunately, he gets to accompany me to work more often than not. He brings joy to my workplace. More importantly, he is helping me as I work through a challenging time. The sudden loss of my husband was the biggest shock I have ever had to endure in my life. I still haven't let go of his belongings, but when that time comes, Buckley will be there for me.

We have continued to work, and Buckley is making great strides as a service dog. He is intelligent, kind, loving, spunky and a bit mischievous, too. He brings me joy, and I am blessed to have him. I cannot adequately express my gratitude to Matt and Kristine! They have truly become best friends, and we will all continue this journey together.

CHAPTER 15

BEAUTIFUL BONDING AND LOVE: MY JOURNEY WITH BIANCA ROSE

Yvonne Thornton

I have been diagnosed with multiple medical conditions to include vertigo, sleep apnea, and high blood pressure. Three years ago, after the passing of my first service dog, I felt another service dog would benefit me with my numerous health conditions, and to provide medical alerts.

After much research, my instinct led me to contact an ethical Poodle breeder in New Jersey. I carefully explained my medical needs and what I was looking for in the puppy who would become my service dog. Based on pictures of the litter, I picked "Purple Girl." When the Neurological Stimulation Workup placed her as the perfect match for my needs, I knew this was the beginning of a meant-to-be journey.

Until my Purple Girl was old enough to be brought home to me; I called her breeder often and asked to put the phone to my puppy's ears to hear my voice. Purple Girl wasn't a real name, so after changing her name to Bianca Rose, I asked the breeder to use her name as frequently as possible.

Weeks felt like years until finally, the long-anticipated day to pick up my Bianca Rose arrived. When I walked into the breeder's house, only an adult Standard Poodle approached me. I expected my puppy.

I asked, "Where is my Bianca Rose?"

Creating one of my life's most impactful moments, little Bianca Rose bounded around the corner, jumped into my arms, and kissed my face all over. The tears I cried, my overwhelming emotions, and a silent realization that everything would be okay flooded me. I knew this was the beginning of a powerful journey.

While the trip home lasted 18 hours, sitting in the back of the truck with Bianca Rose seemed to last only a few short minutes to me. Together, we began our beautiful bonding and love story. While I could not fully imagine or articulate what the pathway would be, I felt a deep inner sense of hope, optimism, and healing.

I immediately immersed myself in training Bianca Rose. I sought every piece of advice I could find, plus the help of reputable trainers, including my long-time friend, Matt Burgess from Freedom Fidos. Mutual love, respect, and admiration form the basis of Bianca Rose's and my relationship. Additionally, we almost seem to read each other's minds.

Bianca Rose passed her Canine Good Citizenship (CGC) test at 11-months-old. Her ability to learn, comprehend, and retain knowledge is astounding. I believe a secure and loving connection like we have amplifies her talents and skills.

During Bianca Rose's training, I inadvertently discovered that she prefers her commands given in French. I found this comical and had a lightbulb moment when it occurred to me that she is, after all, a French Poodle.

Bianca Rose has taken on so many roles for me, including mobility aid, alert, and life-saver. While I have both a walker and wheelchair due to my serious mobility issues and vertigo, I was determined to get past the use of those medical instruments. I preferred Bianca Rose to become the medical device of choice.

Bianca Rose alerts me when my blood pressure reaches dangerous extremes, whether too high or too low. She learned this through a combination of training and the connection we have. She even alerted my friend when her blood pressure was out of balance.

Bianca Rose amazingly chooses the appropriate action to help my mobility and prevent me from falling. She does this in a variety of ways. She helps me either by sitting between my legs, putting paws up on my shoulders to steady me or by bracing my legs.

I now have the confidence to go out in public without using an inanimate medical object, such as a wheelchair or walker. Because of Bianca Rose, I have experienced healing, self-empowerment, and improvements in my life in numerous indescribable ways.

My beautiful dog has also saved my life. Sleeping is always of concern to me, because of sleep apnea. I have read numerous circumstances of individuals with this condition passing away in their sleep. One day, when I fell asleep, Bianca Rose once again found the perfect actions required to save my life. She threw a tennis ball in my face, licked my face, and alerted my husband.

My amazing companion also provides life-saving support when my bradycardia makes my heart rate drop. When dizziness and sickness ail me, I am now confident I have help. Recently, when I was helping with set-up at our community center, I called Bianca Rose out of a down-stay position to help me. She responded immediately by bracing me with her paws on my shoulders. Before her, I would have fallen on the floor. Even if she can't prevent me from falling, she helps me. When I recently fell, she stood over me, guarding me until help arrived.

While Bianca Rose is only 2-year- old, the numerous ways she has saved my life and empowered me to feel like a lifetime. She knows me in a way that no others do. Bianca Rose knows every time I am out of balance in any way. And, like all canines, she seeks to restore me to balance. She alerts me to oncoming dizziness, sickness, or mobility impairments, often long before I am aware of the imminent problems.

I used to stay at home most of the time. However, Bianca Rose has empowered me to return to going out in public and having a social life with confidence. Previously, this would have created fear for me. Because of Bianca Rose, I am once again able to live my life's purpose with a dedication to helping humanity.

Our journey together is beyond description. Bianca Rose helped me turn fear into confidence, embarrassment into pride, and discouragement into empowerment. Before her, I had become sheltered at home. Now, I am driven to live my life and empower others.

Accepting the invitation from Matt Burgess with Freedom Fidos to become one of their Service Dog Handler Teams was an incredible honor for me. My goal: helping future Service Dog Handler Teams to receive the same life-changing, healing, impactful journey, and a connection as Bianca Rose and I have always experienced.

I know our journey will be a long, fulfilling one with numerous ripple effects for myself, her, and others.

Dedication to my husband, Ron, my prince charming, and my amazing service dog, Bianca Rose.

CHAPTER 16

HOW MY DOG SHOWED ME
MY LIFE PURPOSE

Matt Burgess

I served in the military for eight years with deployments to Bosnia, Macedonia, and Iraq. During those deployments, I experienced four blast explosions, creating *Traumatic Brain Injury* as well as a reaction to anthrax. These incidents also resulted in 18 previously non-existent medical conditions.

While at Walter Reed Army Hospital and undergoing a sleep study; I was asked to take a large amount of Ambien. Much like the date rape drugs, this made me conscious, yet, powerless to stop the male sleep technician from making me become his next victim.

I was medically retired from the military in 2006. Two years later, after losing my house, cars, and good credit rating, I received a 100% permanent and total VA Disability Rating as well as Combat-Related Special Compensation.

In 2012, while enrolled at the University of Georgia(UGA), my long-time pet of 15 years passed away. Consequently, I decided to go to the Athens Animal Shelter in Georgia to see if I could find another dog to adopt. When I walked into the first kennel, a little, fluffy brown and black bundle of fur ran up and started chewing my shoelaces, almost as he was pleading with me, "Please, take me!"

I applied to adopt that little bundle of joy; and despite the waiting list of six individuals in front of me, the shelter approved me instead.

During his first year as an untrained pup, Brinks immediately started waking me up at night; and saving my life when I would remove my CPAP mask. I'd stop breathing up to 13 times per minute.

In 2013, pet dog Brinks, already doing life-saving tasks for me, elevated himself to an even higher level. While I was building a privacy fence, the wind blew a board loose. It hit me in the head, knocking me unconscious. Brinks jumped an existing five-foot wire fence wall, scratched on the neighbor's door, alerting her to a problem, and jumped back over the wall to me. I woke up to Brinks, dropping my cell phone on my chest and licking my face. In that defining, powerful, transformative, and life-saving moment, Brinks let me know what our life's purpose was to be. We planned to start a service dog organization to rescue dogs from shelters and task-train them to be life-saving, healing, and medical instrument of service dogs for disabled veterans at no cost to them. We believed we could not withhold the indescribable healing and empowerment we had experienced from this more-than-deserving population.

Subsequently, I found a South Carolina based service dog organization, which stated they would train Brinks to be a service dog. During my time at this organization, I realized I had a gift for training and connecting with canines. Therefore, I trained Brinks to be a task-trained service dog, following guidelines of the Americans with Disabilities Act, in addition to becoming one of the organizations primary trainers.

About Freedom Fidos

Consistent with the life purpose Brinks had previously shown me, we co-founded Freedom Fidos in 2014. After receiving our IRS 501(C)(3), non-profit approval rating in South Carolina, Freedom Fidos spent two years there. Then, the organization moved to Georgia. Fidos4Heroes ((DBA) Freedom Fidos) received our IRS 501(C)(3) approval rating in addition to our Georgia Corporation letter in September 2016.

Freedom Fidos purchased the property that is now the location of their facility in November 2016.

Freedom Fidos had been empowering lives from its inception five years ago. With 50 service dog-teams, the organization began changing the lives of many servicemen and women who suffer from disabilities attained during their time of service. Just as these veterans proudly volunteered to serve their country, the organization run by volunteers is giving back to our nation's heroes.

The organization inspired handlers from home-bound to never home, frightened to fearless, powerless to empowered, from sick to mostly well and have witnessed loners become leaders.

The countless resiliency stories of the human spirit which we witness on a repeated basis could fill a book. These stories continuously make every member of the organization thank Brinks for being the first voice to let us know our calling and commission. We watch nature's ultimate healers collaborate with the determination of our handlers; to keep serving their communities provides us with a never-ending sense of purpose and fulfillment. It gives us an unquenchable desire to do more. We are committed to making a difference as we save the lives of canines and veterans.

Dedication to my friends, Dan Sidles and Danny Agers.

CHAPTER 17

WRONG REASON, RIGHT OUTCOME
Scott Siegel

I am a 62-year-old USAF Vietnam War veteran, and I lost my eyesight ten years ago due to *diabetes* and *glaucoma*. My original reason for getting a guide dog was purely selfish. My condo didn't allow pets so I would beat them at their own game. I received my first guide, Tony, a black Labrador Retriever, 25 months ago, from Guide Dog Foundation for the Blind (GDF). This organization also supplies various service dogs to veterans under their division called America's Vetdogs.

I was initially expecting to go to their campus in Smithtown, New York, on Long Island. Plans changed the first time when they stated they wanted me to participate in the program "CATS and Dogs" at the Veterans Blind Rehabilitation Center in Biloxi, Mississippi. In this program, they pair up two veterans who each have training with a dog four hours a day and learn some Computer Aided Technology (CATS) the other four hours. As luck would have it, the other veteran couldn't get away from his home life to attend, so the school decided that I would train at home.

I met the instructor and my dog, Tony, on a Friday night at my condo. My instructor, Steve, and I decided we would start training the next afternoon after my local National Federation of the Blind (NFB) meeting, where Steve would talk about the school to our members.

On Saturday, we worked on basic commands, how much to feed and water, a relieving schedule, and how to apply the harness and remove it. Steve then left until Monday so Tony and I could bond and be familiar with each other.

On Monday, we worked on routes close to home, modifying them to make us a safer working team. Some of my travel routes were in my apartment complex's parking lot and the driveway. I wasn't aware before when Steve showed me a more reliable path to walk, which was slightly longer but less time in areas that cars frequent.

Each day of the week, we reinforced what we had already done and added more. We worked on bus travel, both types of buses I usually ride, the train, grocery shopping, and several trips to Walmart. We even went to a movie where I learned that Tony was quick and could grab my snack of mozzarella cheese sticks in the blink of an eye. Near the end of the training, we worked on crossing some major eight-lane intersections. Throughout the training, Steve was extremely professional, and we covered all the required topics.

On the last day, we completed the paperwork, transferring ownership of Tony to me. I understood that I would receive the next bag of dog food free, and all I had to do was contact the maker, Nature's Select. When I did, I found out that graduates of GDF will continue to get food at a discounted price.

I moved into a different complex last year, and Tony has adapted to the new location. He has befriended all my neighbors and their pets. No matter what Tony is doing, if he sees me pick up his harness, he runs to me and is ready to go to work. The only place I don't take him is to my golf lessons because he thinks he should retrieve my golf ball and return it to me. I think he is unhappy when he sees me take out my golf clubs. Tony is a real trooper who needs minimal correction, stays focused on guiding me, and we have a great bond.

I found out Tony really likes to swim, although I don't think my friend's pool will ever be free of fur again. He can be a pig, though. My roommate has a Rottweiler, and if she leaves her door open for a few minutes, Tony will run in and finish her dog's food. Tony does travel on long trips quite well; he went with me to two conventions, both by plane and Amtrak. We are planning a trip to Costa Rica soon.

Tony has made a significant impact on my life, and I look forward to many adventures that we will share soon. I believe that we are to the point that I don't even have to give a command on what direction I want to go, just a slight pressure on his harness and he will take me there. He really is my best friend, and I hope we have many more good years working together.

To my father, who saw a difference that my service dog, Tony, has made in my life.

CHAPTER 18

MILITARY AND AUTISM

The Jopling Family

The Jopling family was established in 2007 when Josh and Kristin were married. Before the marriage, Josh had served four years as a commissioned officer in the Army with one deployment to Iraq in 2005-2006 as a 1st LT and Platoon leader in Sadr City, Iraq. You may have heard about the National Geographic series called "The Long Road Home," which tells the story of what happened in Sadr during Josh's deployment there.

Josh got out of the military and met Kristin and her son, Rafe during that time. He worked for a home building company for one year and then decided the civilian life wasn't for him. With a new family, Josh decided to re-enter the Army during the Surge. He entered as a Captain in August 2007 and received orders to report to Fort Knox immediately.

After attending the captain's career course in Fort Knox, Kentucky, Josh and his family moved to Fort Hood, Texas in 2008 was assigned with the 1st Cavalry. They were expecting a new baby; then Josh is notified he would deploy to Iraq in December of 2008.

Bryson, whom we wish for to have a service dog, was born October 2, 2008, in Temple, Texas, two months before Josh would have to deploy for a year.

During Josh's deployment to Iraq, Kristin received news from their family doctor that their first son, Rafe, was diagnosed with *Asperger's syndrome*. It was a complete shock, and Josh came home on rest and recuperation (R&R) to help the family adjust to the new diagnosis. It was their first introduction into the world of *autism*. They were able to set up the therapies their son would need, and Josh returned to Iraq to finish out his deployment.

Josh finished his company command in November 2010; he transferred to Schofield Barracks in Hawaii to work as a trainer/mentor for the National Guard and Reserves at Barber's Point. Josh deployed twice to the Philippines on short tours to train Philippine forces to fight against insurgents. In Hawaii, Josh, as a Casualty Notification Officer, was assigned to a family of a soldier killed in Afghanistan. He was to escort the widow to Dover Air Force to receive the casket. Because there were not enough trained officers, Josh was also assigned to be the Casualty Assistance Officer for the family. It was one of the hardest assignments he's ever had to do.

Josh was not deployed long term during their time in Hawaii; he still spent many nights away from the family on temporary assignments and field training (TDY). While stationed in Hawaii, the Jopling adopted their daughter from Ethiopia in 2013. It was then that they started seeing signs of *autism* in Bryson.

While Josh was in school, the family saw a psychiatrist off-base to test Bryson for *autism* and to continue to treat their oldest son with *Asperger's*. They received a diagnosis of *Moderate Autism and Impulsive Mood Disorder*. Bryson struggled with everyday tasks and could not cope with change. We received news that Josh will be deployed to Guatemala in 2014 for a year as an advisor to counter-narcotics units. Kristin and the children moved back to Fort Hood, Texas, so her parents would be able to help.

During this deployment, Bryson was admitted to a mental health hospital because he could not cope with the new changes in his life. It was especially hard on Bryson being away from his father yet again. Josh came home on emergency leave and was able to get Bryson situated on a new medication to help with his anxiety.

It is when the family started looking into the possibility of a service dog for their son. Being denied on every application and inquiry to request a service dog was simply unjust. Kristin has researched and contacted many organizations for two years, and to be turned away time after time.

In the past three years, Josh has been away for a total of 23 months. In his almost 16 years of service, Josh has been deployed long term four times, not to mention the many times he went on TDY for weeks or months. It has dramatically impacted the family, especially Bryson. As of July 2019, The Jopling family, currently stationed at Fort Riley, Kansas, where Josh is Division Command Inspector General! They hope to have a break in deployments while they are there.

Hoping for a service dog were ever going to happen we were ecstatic when Freedom Fidos stated they would train a service dog for Bryson. We received a call from the Boyd Family; to let us know how they were planning to give up their Christmas presents in 2017, and to sponsor a service dog for Bryson. We were so profoundly humbled. Dutch, a Goldendoodle, which Freedom Fidos trained, has benefited our son by providing security and emotional support during anxiety attacks. Dutch is providing a calming benefit in boosting his confidence and redirecting his moods.

Bryson gets overwhelmed with public places being too loud or crowded, and too cold or hot. We often do not go anywhere because of this but having a service dog has helped to intervene at the onset of a meltdown so we can continue our outings. If the sun gets too bright for Bryson Dutch provides mobility support, which allows Bryson to walk outside until his eyes can adjust. It helps Bryson to remain independent, and a big thanks to Dutch.

Bryson struggles to take a shower when the water is too much for him, so having a service dog redirects Bryson's focus and make showers more bearable. While Bryson has insomnia and is up during the middle of the night without our knowledge, his service dog would lead Bryson back to his bed safely.

We are so thankful for Bryson's task-trained service dog, Dutch, gifted by Freedom Fidos. Without Freedom Fidos' generous gift – Bryson would not be making progress he is currently attaining. Thank you, Freedom Fidos, for all you have done for my family!

My Humble Tributes:

I refer Dan Sidles and Danny Agers as 'warped angels amongst us" despite their inability to overcome the challenges, which, ultimately shortened their life, while deeply impacting mine. Not only is my heart broken, daily, I miss them. They saved my life. They made me a better person, and it was they who encouraged me to serve humanity through the use of nature's ultimate healers: service dogs.

While Joshua Burgess only lived 17 physical years, the life of his, he REALLY LIVED daily created a far-reaching impact. He made the world a better place in addition to leaving many individuals, and indeed myself, an inspirational blueprint to follow, which demonstrates the incredible power of love for all humanity.

PART 5

PROFESSIONAL LIFE,
A NEW OUTLOOK

CHAPTER 19

SO, WHAT'S THE BIG DEAL ABOUT COLE, THE SEARCH DOG?
Roxanne Bauman

C ole is a 7-year-old black Labrador Retriever who is trained to find live human victims, whether they are lost, hurt, unconscious, or trapped. Cole can skillfully locate victims anywhere and will bark where he thinks the most potent source of the scent. He can target scent in buildings, in collapsed building rubble, in snow, water, mud, and even outside as far away as a half a mile.

Cole is an air -scenting dog that looks for live victims and does not require an article of clothing to find a victim. There are other similar working dogs such as: Cadaver Dogs (specialize in locating dead victims), Wilderness Dogs (specialize in wide area searches), Avalanche Dogs (specialize in snow and rescue), Tracking Dogs (nose to the ground and may require a scent article), Patrol Dogs (specialize in finding and apprehending criminals), Arson Dogs (determine intentionally set fires), and Narcotic Dogs (determine presence of drugs).

Some dogs can have more than one specialty and will require extra training in addition to their regular daily training. This, however, is an uncommon discovery.

Cole and Engineer/Paramedic, Roxanne Bauman, are a canine/handler team that belongs to the Utah Task Force I (UT-TF1), based out of West Jordan, Utah. Currently, there are 28 Task Force Teams in the US. Utah has one of those limited teams. UT-TF1 has deployed teams to national disasters such as 9/11,

Hurricane Katrina, Colorado flooding, Utah flooding, and Hurricane Harvey.

Not only is Cole a tremendous national resource, but he also works in Davis County and regionally throughout the state when there is a local emergency. UT-TF1 has over 200+ members and has the self-sustain its 70-member team for 72 hours without any outside assistance during a deployment. The Task Force has eight certified FEMA Type-I canines and two Human Remains (Cadaver) Canine/Handler Teams.

(For more information about UT-TF1, go to
http://www.utahtaskforce1.org
or FEMA Search and Rescue, go to
http://www.fema.gov/urban-search-rescue)

Cole was born in California. He was brought into El Dorado County Animal Shelter and originally named Bouncer because he would jump up and down all day long. During his first interview for adoption, they could tell Cole had too much energy to be a pet. The shelter called the National Disaster Search Dog Foundation (NDSDF) in Ojai, California, to see if he would qualify. He did! Cole passed all the preliminary tests with flying colors.

The Search Dog Foundation's mission is to rescue dogs from shelters and train them to be rescuers themselves. Once accepted into the program, whether or not they pass the training, these dogs will never have to be rescued again and guaranteed to a loving home. They are trained for 9-12 weeks and paired with a handler at no cost. Normally, if purchased from a private breeder and with much less training, these dogs cost around $9,000. After they are FEMA Certified, their estimated worth is approximately $25,000. (For more information about NDSDF located in Santa Barbara, California, go to http://www.searchdogfoundation.org)

Cole trained at the Search Dog Foundation for nine-months and was then paired with Roxanne in December 2013. He and three other dogs (Decker, Taylor, and Tanner) came to Utah to work with their new handlers. Cole lives with Roxanne and works on duty with her at the Layton Fire Department. He is the first FEMA type dog to work in Davis County, and his first shift was December 18, 2013. And, yes, he even had to work on Christmas Day.

At Cole's most recent certification process, he was able to target three victims at 1-minute, 5-minutes and 10-minutes respectively in an area called "the pile." The pile is a 15,000 square foot area, and frequently 10-feet deep. Each dog has to recertify every three years to maintain their FEMA Type II (FSA) and Type I (CE) certifications. Spring of 2020 will be Cole's last re-certification; he will be set to retire at 11-years-old.

Cole has adopted a skill as a stress reliever for the firefighter crew. There was an incident where a firefighter separated from the crew for some time. Once the firefighter was safe, this person held onto Cole for a half-hour for comfort.
Cole is a fantastic PR asset for Layton Fire Department, Utah, including many surrounding cities and states.

Survival tips

Establishing priorities if you are lost, especially if you are lost long-term, is one of the first steps to survival. Basic needs are food, fire, shelter, and water. Shelter is usually required first, but this can depend on where you are and individual circumstances. An adult can survive for three weeks without food, but only three days without water. Never wait until you run out of water before you look for more. Conserve your supplies. Remember that the human body loses 4-6 pints of water each day. Loss of liquids through respiration and perspiration increases with work rate and temperature. It must be replaced by actual water or water contained in food. You can retain fluids and keep loss to a minimum by avoiding exertion, not smoking, keeping cool, staying in shade, not lying on hot ground, eating as little as possible, breathing through the nose and not drinking any alcohol.

Considering all of the above, always attempt to remain in the area in which you were first "lost" to make it easier for the rescue party and the specially trained canine to locate you.

CHAPTER 20

PUZZLE PIECES

DeAnna Moore

At times, our lives come together like pieces of a puzzle. Some parts we cannot fully comprehend until the picture becomes entirely complete.

In 2013, I was a retired veterinarian teaching anatomy and physiology at a local community college. I was also dealing with long-standing, advanced eye diseases (*uveitis* and *glaucom*a) secondary to *juvenile rheumatoid arthritis*. This disease had been a part of my life since I was 19 months of age. In addition to multiple joint problems, this foe had taken my right eye and had my doctors in a constant battle to save vision in my left.

During this period, on a chance Google search of Eli Manning, my husband found that Eli is a supporter of Guiding Eyes for the Blind (GEB) in New York. A bit more research and my husband, Andrew, discovered Guiding Eyes had a puppy raising region very near our home. We both felt this was an excellent opportunity to volunteer as it involved both animals and helping others with vision loss. They are two of my great passions.

Fast forward a few months, and we found ourselves raising our first pup, named Peppy for Guiding Eyes. Much to our amazement, the first photo we saw of Peppy nestled comfortably in the arms of Eli Manning! Little did I know how profoundly this puppy raising experience would impact our lives. A puzzle piece had just slipped quietly into place.

Raising Peppy taught me so much about relationships. The commitment, trust, and consistency needed to create the deep bonds required for a life-long partnership. In many ways, Peppy and I matured together. I grew into a more confident, skilled raiser while he transformed from a small puppy into an amazing, brilliant young adult right before our eyes. Andrew and I also learned first-hand about the "heart of the puppy-raiser." What a commitment of work, time, and love is required of these volunteers! The willingness to give so freely and let go for the good of another still inspires us to this day.

As we were raising Bradley, our second GEB puppy, the cornea transplant in my only sighted eye quite unexpectedly began to fail. As my vision began to decline rapidly, one of the greatest fears of my life was coming true. However, the puzzle pieces of my life were coming together beautifully. I realized something from my experience as a raiser. I could now see the possibility of a rewarding and purpose-filled life where vision loss is only a part of who I am, but does not define me. I was finally wiggling free of the fear of blindness that had me gripped in its talons for a very long time.

In February of 2016, I found myself involved with Guiding Eyes in a brand-new capacity. I was a student in the February class. I was flown to New York to the Guiding Eyes campus to be a part of the three-week residential program. These were three of the most wonderful, challenging, amazing, and exhausting weeks of my life. My big-hearted, beautiful yellow girl, Kendalee, entered my life. When I became aware of Kendalee's name, I immediately realized I was friends with one of her raisers. Wow, what a small world!

Seven other residential students and three amazing trainers became fast friends as we worked alongside each other during long hours over the following weeks. The growth of our Guide teams was a fantastic process to witness.

Kendalee is much more than a "dog" or a "mobility aid" to me. She is a beautiful soul. When I pick up her harness, it feels like taking the hand of a dear and trusted friend.

It has not always been an easy journey, especially those

first months at home away from the supervision and advice of trainers by our side. Although there was an immediate connection and respect for one another, we were awkward at first. Think of a young new couple learning to dance for the first time. This guide/handler relationship depends on trust. Also, as in any relationship, whether canine-human or human-human, trust is not instantaneous. It is earned and requires time. There have been days I know I let Kendalee down. There have been days she has disappointed me. However, this does not mean we, as a team, have failed. I would say these are perhaps the days we have grown the most.

With Kendalee by my side, I have become more optimistic and more confident. All in all, a better version of myself. I am so very grateful every single day for this life-changing soul wrapped in a gorgeous coat of yellow fur. I look forward to adding many more pieces to our puzzle as we continue building our lives as a Guiding Eyes Team.

I want to dedicate my chapter to all of our wonderful puppy-raisers. Thank you for giving freely of your time, and for sharing a portion of your hearts with our amazing dogs.

CHAPTER 21

RAISING FOR A REASON

Vicki Heckman

I have always loved dogs. From the time I can remember, I have always loved puppies. I grew up in Scottsdale, Arizona, and only had a dog for a few months while we were growing up. After college, I worked two additional jobs to supplement my teaching salary. I was a nanny in the evening and weekends for a fantastic family who simply loved animals. They had multiple dogs, a cat, a bird, and even a lizard. I helped to care for the animals as part of my essential responsibilities with the family. They decided to add a puppy to the family. A very special puppy. It was a Canine Companions for Independence (CCI) puppy that would be puppy-raised and trained to be a future service dog. I fell in love with the puppy and the program. I knew that one day when I had a family of my own, I would also raise puppies for the same organization.

Canine Companions for Independence is a fantastic organization that provides highly trained assistance dogs and ongoing support to people with disabilities. These dogs matched with adults, children, and veterans are free of charge. CCI offers four types of assistance dogs. Service dogs serve adults with physical disabilities by performing daily tasks; and hearing dogs paired with people who are deaf or are hard of hearing. Facility dogs work with people with special needs in education, health care, or any approved group setting. Finally, skilled companion dogs are carefully assigned are with children or adults with physical, cognitive, and developmental disabilities. Fast forward several years from when I was a nanny, and my family and I are honored to be puppy-raisers for this organization.

Before being a stay at home mom, I was a first-grade teacher. I would spend the school year teaching and preparing the students with the skills they would need in the future. At the end of the year, I would send them prepared to their second-grade class; and I would start the process all over again in the fall with a new group of students. Puppy-raising isn't that different for me. We send the 18-month-old puppy off for Advanced Training and start fresh with a new 8-week-old puppy.

I find that being a puppy-raiser for Canine Companions for Independence is the perfect way to combine my love of dogs and my love of volunteering and giving back. It is also an excellent way for us to provide an example to our children as we do our best to teach them about giving to others. My family is blessed to be in the position to be able to make a charitable donation to an organization. We have chosen to make our donation in the form of raising puppies in our home for CCI. Each puppy lives with us from the time he is eight-weeks-old until he is approximately 18 to 22-months-old. We provide our time, resources, financial support, and love to this puppy before turning him in for Advanced Training. The process is even more rewarding than I could have ever imagined. We are currently raising our fourth puppy and plan to puppy-raise many more in the future.

Being a puppy-raiser covers a wide variety of emotions. There are pride and joy when the puppy has an outstanding day out in public. It can be frustrating and disappointing when we thought the puppy was fully housebroken, and to discover that was not the case. There is always great excitement and anticipation, waiting for the arrival of the eight-weeks-old puppy, and there is sadness and heartache when the puppy is turned in for Advanced Training. Above all else, there is hope. We have confidence that we will raise a puppy that will change someone's life

The puppy-raising program begins with an application and interview. Once approved, our family waits for the notification revealing the date our puppy will arrive, the gender, the breed, and the name. It feels like Christmas when we receive that news. Our role requires quite a bit of patience. We need to prepare the puppy for Advanced Training by providing a variety of socialization opportunities, new experiences, attending weekly obedience classes, and exposure to new sounds, people, and textures.

Our primary role is to prepare the dog for Advanced Training with professional trainers and to provide a strong foundation. It includes ensuring the puppy always feels safe and confident. We have to evaluate new experiences to avoid overexcited behaviors or fearful responses from the puppy. When the puppy is old enough, we begin to take him with us to age-appropriate places such as a park or a child's baseball game. It allows him the opportunity to be exposed to new people and sounds but gives us a chance for him to learn in a less structured environment. Eventually, the puppy will be mature enough and ready to practice walking by our side in a store or laying under a table in a restaurant. We have to be careful to provide opportunities for learning success and never take the puppy somewhere that would be too challenging or overwhelming.

We are also responsible for teaching the puppy 30 commands that the professional trainers will refine to train the dogs the skills they will need to become service dogs. I am always amazed how quickly these CCI puppies can learn a new command. The puppies love learning, and with each new puppy, I am learning to become a better trainer for them. Our 30 commands are what the trainers build on to train the dogs the skills to be service dogs. For example, we teach the puppies to walk backwards. The trainers teach them to open a drawer while walking backward. We teach the puppies the "up" command, and the trainers teach them to turn on a light switch with the same movement.

As our children are growing up, they can help with the training of the puppies more often. They were very young when we raised our first puppy, and most of the tasks fell on the shoulders of mine or my husband's. Now they can walk the puppies, take them outside, put them in the kennel, feed them, and so much more. I love hearing them explain that we are raising a puppy for someone else, and the puppy could help improve the quality of that person's life.

There is a massive sense of pride in watching the puppy transform from a tiny, silly 8-week-old to a confident, prepared 18-month-old. It is incredible to see the unique personality of each puppy develop. One puppy would put himself to bed in its kennel promptly at 8:30 pm each night while another puppy would prefer to spend its time stretching and rolling in an opened kennel before joining the family in the morning. The joy I receive from this process is difficult to explain. Many don't understand how we can "give up" the puppy, but we know that someone else needs that puppy more than us. There is another side of puppy-raising that is more difficult than the training, and it is the part of the process that people ask me about most frequently. Turning in the puppy at 18-months is a bittersweet day for our family. We invest a lot of time and love in these puppies, and we are so full of hope that they will go on to change someone's life. Saying goodbye is very difficult, but it is something we are prepared for as it is part of the program. Each puppy we raise leaves a lasting impression on our hearts. The fact is that only 40-50% of the puppies that begin the program will go on to graduate. As the puppy-raiser, we receive monthly reports from the professional trainers. We wait for these reports and hope that we have done enough and hope that the puppy we raised has the drive and determination to do what it takes to graduate. We have no contact with the puppy we raised during their time in Advanced Training. They work with professional trainers to refine and advance their skills for six to nine months.

The first puppy we raised did not graduate from the program. It was heartbreaking. We had put so much into that puppy, but we knew to go in that the chances were less than half that he would graduate. After each time we turn in a dog, I replay our time with the puppy in my head and hope that we did enough to prepare him for his future. The six months of professional training is a long time to hold out hope and wait. Puppy-raising takes a lot of patience, even when the puppy no longer lives with us.

Our second puppy went on to successfully graduate from Advanced Training and is currently working as a Skilled Companion Dog in November 2017. We were honored to pass the pup's leash to a 19-year-old young man, and our love for the organization and their mission grew even stronger.

We went through the entire process again with a third puppy. We went through the ups and downs of raising a puppy, and the heartache and hope when handing him over to the professional trainers. Sadly, after several months in Advanced Training, our third puppy decided that working life was not for him. That phone call is nothing short of devastating as a puppy-raiser. Although these dogs have to demonstrate the very best behavior, skills, and temperament, it is still so disappointing to receive the news that the dog we raised will not graduate. We are currently raising our fourth puppy and have high hopes for his future.

A puppy-raiser has the opportunity to adopt the dog they raised if the dog does not graduate. At that point, the dog would be a family pet. All other dogs, released from the program, will be placed by CCI with an approved family for adoption.

Through this journey as a puppy-raiser, we have met some incredible people. Unfortunately, there are no other puppy-raisers within a two-hour radius of our home, but I am hopeful that will change one day. There is a vast online community of puppy-raisers and graduates that provide endless support and advice. I have met puppy-raisers who have raised 25 puppies, so I start with them when I have a question. I have met graduates with their service dogs and seen these amazing animals at work. Finally, I have met so many people who are interested in learning more about this incredible program.

When a puppy we have raised graduates, we attend a graduation ceremony and have the opportunity to meet the person placed with the puppy we raised. I think about that experience when I'm standing outside in sub-zero temperatures with a new puppy hoping they will go potty. I remind myself of how important these dogs are for someone else. When the new puppy cries during the night, I remind myself that we are teaching our children to be more selfless. I remember the life-changing experience it was to pass the leash of the puppy we raised to his new partner. I hope to pass many more leashes in the future.

I dedicate this story to the amazing Canine Companions for Independence graduates, volunteers, and staff I have met on this puppy raising journey.

CHAPTER 22

ONE STEP AT A TIME

Brian McKenna

My name is Brian McKenna, and since as far back as I can remember, my brother has been blind. He lost his sight at age five, and he is three and a half years older than me. Blindness is something I've been around my entire life. Being Pat's little brother has most definitely prepared me for my career as an instructor at The Seeing Eye (TSE). My family has always been aware The Seeing Eye located just twenty miles from our home. It wasn't until Pat went to law school in Newark, New Jersey, that he felt he was ready to get his first dog guide.

At that time, I was just about to graduate college up in Vermont and was pretty unsure about the road that lay ahead. I knew that an active lifestyle was a must and that I very much enjoyed helping others. My degree was in English, and I had aspirations of becoming a teacher, but I had no idea in which venue and stage. Pat's experience at The Seeing Eye was reassurance I needed that applying to be an instructor at The Seeing Eye. It would be a perfect fit for me, and, indeed, it was.

Once hired in October of 2004, I quickly learned just how challenging and in-depth my apprenticeship was going to be. The apprentice program is a three-year on-site training regimen designed to prepare apprentices for their continual evolving careers as instructors. TSE's apprenticeship program, comprised of all aspects of being a trainer, while being paired with a senior instructor and under the close watch of the Apprentice Supervisor. The first three years, I trained dogs, taught six classes of students, carefully observed TSE senior instructors' lessons, and successfully passed three exams. It certainly tested my retention of everything I was learning.

In July of 2016, I was honored and humbled with the promotion to Master Instructor. Additional responsibilities with this title are apprentice mentorship, outreach demonstrations, and presentations, more time on the road visiting graduates and applicants during the dog training cycle and taking on various assignments deemed challenging. This job is the perfect career for me, and honestly, genuinely what I was meant to do.

As I reflect today, I am so amazed at how quickly the years have gone. In October of 2017, I will have completed my 13th-year of training dogs. In those years, I met my best friend at work, married her, and we have two beautiful children. We both have lost several dogs in our twenties; it felt like the last link to our youth. My family shares the great pride I feel in going to work at The Seeing Eye every day. Even if my children are too young too fully grasp the impact these dogs make, they think Daddy working with doggies is pretty cool.

The first day with new dogs is always exciting. You never know what you're going to get! My job is cyclical, and it never gets old. We receive anywhere from six to eight 18-month-old dogs roughly one week after we complete teaching a class. TSE's incredible selfless puppy-raisers' primary role is to socialize our pups, housebreak them, teach them basic obedience, and provide for them a loving and supportive family environment. The breakdown of this new group, or string, of dogs, is usually half female, half male and an even mix of German Shepherds, Labrador Retrievers, Golden Retrievers, and Labrador-Golden crosses.

I am one of four instructors on our team, and there are five teams. Each team is at a different point of training. Examples: one team would be in the first month of training, and the other three teams would be at various points of training. The fifth team would be teaching a class with fully trained and qualified Seeing Eye Dogs. Anywhere from 20 to 23 students are invited to live on our campus in Morristown, New Jersey, to be paired with their new Seeing Eye Dogs. It is a challenging and emotional time, but so profound, powerful, and rewarding.

We have four months to train our wonderful four-legged friends, but additional time is always an option. About 60% of our dogs successfully make it through the program, and that figure is pretty much the same for the breeds and genders we train. All dogs, like people, are different and variations of teaching styles, not to mention patience, are needed. Our dogs must successfully demonstrate their ability in these areas: to stop for curbs, avoid obstacles, watch out for traffic, ignore the temptations from other animals and people, and behave appropriately in all situations. As instructors, we are expected to test our dogs' abilities as guides by wearing blindfolds at the two-month and four-month period of their training with our supervisors close behind.

Throughout the four-month training cycle, we are expected to travel a minimum of two weeks to visit our graduates and applicants in their home environments anywhere throughout North America. We transfer full ownership of our dogs; we provide this follow up service to assist our graduates with any issues or challenges. Some examples: Learn a new route to work, to assist with an access issue, to evaluate a challenging street crossing, or review the training they received from you. The days and weeks on the road have taught me so much more than I ever anticipated. The variables that come into play with dog guide mobility are intricate and unpredictable. I consider myself so blessed to play a role in this process. Our donors, volunteers, graduates, and my fellow employees all inspire me to give my dogs and my students my absolute best every day.

Once our dogs are qualified Seeing Eye Dogs, we invite students to class to receive their perfect match. Teaching class is when we finally get to see all of our hard work pay off. There are 12 classes per year. The breakdown of each is generally half new students and half retrain students who have previously worked with a dog. The age range of our students in class is 18 into their 80's. Our dogs work thoughtfully and cautiously because they are receiving the respect and love that only consistency and trust can provide.

A specific dog for a person received based on their need for a dog; comfortable walking pace and the adequate amount of pull from the harness. Our dogs guide by pulling, and each Seeing Eye Dog guides at a different particular pace and pull. We factor many variables into the matching process, and what is perfect for one may not be ideal for another. It is our students' job to be one hundred percent honest with us regarding what exactly they want in a dog guide. It is our job as instructors to reciprocate that honesty and make the most educated decision we possibly can by evaluating all variables and information. The matching process is by no means a foolproof method, and it is not one to be taken lightly. It can be exhausting, but so rewarding. Handing over a new dog to someone is a moment that is more powerful than words. May I never lack the humility to appreciate the profound enormity of that very moment fully.

I am more than grateful to have discovered this road I have traveled. It has brought me immeasurable happiness and peace. The life lessons and moments of reflection I have experienced have no doubt made me a better son, brother, husband, father, and instructor. I can't imagine any other profession that can combine my desire to teach, my love of dogs, and my affinity for working outdoors. I am fully aware that the work I do does make a difference in peoples' lives, and I am so proud of that. I've seen first-hand the difference these dogs have made in my brother's life, and I am so appreciative of all the people involved with The Seeing Eye.

My dedication is to Ginny and Eddie. Always be fast.

CHAPTER 23

AXEL, THE THERAPY DOG

Cindy Yorgason

I have an Engineering degree and moved to Utah in 1984 to be a quality engineer for the Space Shuttle Program. I left that job in 1995, and after working for several other companies, I left the corporate world. I am also a National Level Bicycle Race Official and get to work events all around the country. In 2005, we decided it was time to get a family dog. Our son had many allergies, so we started to look at hypoallergenic breeds. It is how we discovered the Border Terrier and fell in love with the breed. They are one of the oldest terrier breeds used in the fox hunts. They would ride on the horses until the hounds found the fox and the borders would catch them.

Most states have an organization that certifies therapy animals. My dog, Axel, is a therapy dog certified by one such organization, Intermountain Therapy Animals (ITA). In 2010, being diagnosed with cancer Axel was by my side throughout my treatments. I decided I wanted to pay it forward, and in 2012, we went through the certification process with ITA. A great therapy animal is a matter of the animal having the right personality. It's the owner's willingness to put in the time to become certified and becoming a team to share your pet's love with others. Axel was born with a tender heart and was always top of his class through puppy school. Axel has a little brother, Danzee, who always hears about Axel's day working when we get home. Danzee is only three and is still excitable. He needs to mature and behave before we can see if Danzee can be ITA certified and work as a therapy dog.

There are requirements to become certified with ITA; the first step is for you and your dog to have an interview at their office. They usually have dogs and cats at the office, which allows the staff to see how your dog reacts to other animals. Afterward, there is an all-day seminar for you, and then the next day is testing of your dog. Some of the tests include checking if the dog follows all given commands and does not react when another dog enters the same room. Upon completion of these tests, you shadow someone at the facility you wish to visit, and you and your dog are in turn shadowed to ensure you have an understanding of the facility. If you go to more than one facility, the last two steps must repeat. You also have to retest with your dog every two years to ensure they continue to meet ITA's standards.

I wanted to visit with cancer patients and pay it forward. For us, that meant we would go to Huntsman Cancer Institute in Salt Lake City, Utah. We live in Ogden, about 30 miles north of the city. Every Tuesday, we go down and visit patients in the infusion or hospital rooms. The infusion room is where the patients receive their chemotherapy drugs. Axel has a fantastic sense of who to snuggle in close with or to lay further away. I enjoy being able to visit with the patient and their families. It is a unique opportunity to share my journey with them and celebrate life each year. For cancer patients, there are new dates that become significant milestones, and each milestone is another celebration of life.

In the spring of 2015, a policy regarding therapy animals at McKay-Dee Hospital changed, which meant we would be able to work there and see cancer patients. The hospital is very close to our house, so we started going there on Wednesdays. We visit the waiting areas and the infusion rooms. We have made amazing friends through our weeks of working at the hospital. We love to see these friends, especially when they finish their treatments and been inform they are now cancer-free.

During that same spring, we got the opportunity to join a group of therapy dogs that visit at the Salt Lake City International

Airport. Unlike going to a hospital or other facility, we get to go around as a "pack." It has become one of our favorite days. We have people that look forward to our visits, including airline employees and the TSA. We always look for flights that are delayed and might have stressed-out passengers. We also get to participate in special events at the airport. These include things like the Honor Flights or Snowball Express.

Honor Flights are a fantastic experience, where we get to share our dogs with veterans who are traveling to Washington, D.C., to visit the memorials. We have seen fewer and fewer World War II veterans on subsequent flights while seeing increasing numbers of Korea and Vietnam veterans on these flights. Each veteran has a family member or friend traveling with them. The airport has a big parade and celebration from the moment the veterans arrive until they get onto the plane. The other travelers in the airport always stop and salute these amazing veterans. Some passengers may not realize that their flight would be the Honor Flight. Honor Flights boarding takes longer since the veterans get to board first. We always stay to visit everyone who is waiting and might need a dog visit.

The Snowball Express is a Christmas-time special, where the airline takes Gold Star Families on a special trip. Gold Star families are those with small children that have lost a military parent. Again, the airport goes all out and has Santa for the kids to visit before they board their flight.

Axel usually works three days a week. He gets a bath each week and brushed before every visit. When Axel works, he is quiet and serious, and he saunters. He knows it is time to work when his red leash, collar, and red scarf or vest comes out. Some people even wonder if he likes going, but I assure them that he is always excited when we arrive for work. Axel is a very vocal dog. He "talks" when we park and can't wait to get out of the car.

When we are home, Axel loves to play catch. Axel is a Border Terrier, dogs with strong jaws. He will play tug of the ball at any opportunity with visitors at our house, and he usually wins. When playing with me, he knows to sit and drop it. Over the past few years, Axel has made many friends. He even has his own Facebook page, which allows his friends to watch him work. If you want to follow him, you can find his page at facebook.com/AxelTherapyDog

I know that Axel will not be able to be a therapy dog forever and have started to think ahead to his retirement. I still hope to continue doing work as a Therapy Dog Team and am working with Danzee and thinking about getting another puppy to train as well. Axel has been an amazing dog with an incredibly tender heart. I would love to write an entire book on all the adventures and joy Axel has been able to share.

This chapter is to dedicate to Axel, who passed while the book was in final preparations for release. Axel was an exceptional kid that was born with a tender heart and loved being a Therapy Dog for almost seven years. Axel met thousands of people who just needed a snuggle and love along his journey. He is already greatly missed.

CHAPTER 24

GUIDE DOG USERS

Penny Reeder

Being blind all my life, my first guide dog, Glory, from Fidelco Guide Dog Foundation, came into my life in my fifth decade. My only regret is that I spent those first four-and-a-half decades without experiencing the independence and pleasure of living each day with a guide dog at my side. After Glory came Tess, also a Fidelco Guide Dog, and then Willow, my current guide from The Seeing Eye. Now at age 10, Willow keeps me safe wherever we travel together. Like her predecessors, she brings joy and humor into my life and the lives of our family members and friends.

The second-best blindness-related decision was to search for the companionship and support of other guide dog users. Guide Dog Users, Inc. (GDUI) is the leading advocacy and support group for guide dog users in the United States. The not-for-profit organization provides empathetic peer-support to guide dog users in all stages of their relationships with their dogs. Getting a dog for independence and mobility, they must consider the phase of training and adapt to the guide dog lifestyle by attending a formal guide dog training or self-training. Also, to adjust the day-to-day reality of living with a 24-hour canine companion and integrating that companion into family life, work, and recreation. Finally, when that indispensable guide dog cannot work because of illness, a need to retire, and the inevitable and challenging end of life which none of us can avoid.

GDUI educates the public about interacting with guide dog teams. It advocates on behalf of guide dog users to assure our civil rights protections guaranteed under laws like the Americans with Disabilities Act are protected and enforced. It shares information with members and others about caring for and living with dogs and living well with, and despite, blindness.

I cannot overstate how much owning and working with guide dogs and interacting with so many people within the guide dog community. I smile and swell with pride when I think of my guide dogs and all those connections I have been fortunate to make in our community. I express my appreciation to David Darr, Desmond. O'Neill, Sue Macahill, and all of the former presidents and members at GDUI.

Dedication to my guide dogs: Glory, and Willow – and their wonderful puppy-raisers. Also, the amazing trainers who taught me safe and enhanced independence.

Guide Dog Users, Inc.: Assisting Guide Dog Teams and Advocating for the Civil Rights of People Who Are Blind and Visually Impaired for More Than 40 Years

Guide Dog Users, Inc. (GDUI) advocates for the rights of guide dog users everywhere. Drawing on the experiences and varied knowledge of its members from every region of the USA, GDUI provides peer-support, advocacy and information to the blind and visually impaired members of guide dog teams. In addition, GDUI works with public entities, private businesses and individuals to ensure that guide dog users enjoy the same rights to travel, employment, housing, and participation in all aspects of life that people without disabilities take for granted.

An affiliate of the American Council of the Blind (ACB) since 1972, GDUI is the largest consumer-driven organization of its kind in the world. GDUI sponsors an informative website, provides venues for online discussion and communication, and publishes an award-winning quarterly magazine called

"PawTracks," to share information on matters that resonate with its members and friends.

GDUI maintains a Guide Dog School Survey to facilitate informed choice for everyone who seeks training with a guide dog.

GDUI publishes fact sheets and informational brochures which educate the public on a variety of topics, including the access rights of guide dog teams, and, considering the special danger that uncontrolled dogs can pose to working teams, responsible pet ownership..

We welcome your exploration of our website. And, we provide a fully-staffed toll-free telephone number where experienced guide dog users can answer questions, provide information, share stories, and extend empathetic support.

Guide Dog Users, Inc. Announces Position Statement on the Misrepresentation of Service Animals

The organization's statement is a direct response to the growing epidemic of members of the public passing their pets off as service animals, impeding on the civil rights of those who are blind and rely on legitimate service animals to gain access to public venues.

For Immediate Release

Silver Spring, MD - Guide Dog Users, Inc. (GDUI), the leading organization of blind and visually impaired people who rely on guide dogs as mobility assistants in the United States, has announced its official policy regarding people who attempt to misrepresent their pets as service animals in venues where pets are not generally allowed. The statement aims to inform members of the general public about the civil rights which people who are blind and visually impaired rely upon to guarantee their access to public venues with their guide dogs and to inform business owners about their obligations under the law as well as their rights to deny admittance to animals who do not qualify as legitimate service animals.

"It makes it hard for all of us who depend on our legitimate service animals for independent travel when business owners question our right to visit their establishments in the company of our guide dogs or when untrained or uncontrolled pets masquerading as service animals distract our dogs or make it unsafe for us or our dogs to share the same space," says Penny Reeder of Montgomery Village, Maryland, president of Guide Dog Users, Inc.

Continuing, "The frenzy of nationwide news reports stating that businesses are being inundated with people passing off their pets as service animals has heightened suspicions which makes it even more difficult for individuals with legitimate service animals to access public places. That is why GDUI's Legislative and Advocacy Committees will be focusing on the issues related to the misuse of pets as service animals during the coming months."

Businesses are often unsure of their legal rights and responsibilities when confronted with the need to authenticate whether a service animal is legitimate or "fake." The number of people with hidden disabilities who use service animals has been increasing. And, many people with Emotional Support Animals believe -- mistakenly -- that they have the right to be accompanied by their dogs in all public areas. All of these factors have led to confusion about who has a right to bring a service animal where, what qualifies a dog to be called a service animal, and a steady erosion of public trust.

According to Penny Reeder, "GDUI has developed this official position statement to help businesses and the general public better understand the scope of the problem. The statement includes recommended actions. In addition to helping to educate business owners, GDUI members and affiliates hope to help reduce the number of unruly and aggressive pets in public places by advocating for tougher state laws. There is evidence showing that when businesses post signs warning patrons that misrepresenting service animals is a misdemeanor, complaints about "fake" service animals are significantly reduced. Currently, sixteen United States have either criminal or civil laws against misrepresenting a pet as a service animal. GDUI members and affiliates will be advocating to increase that number.

For more information, visit: http://gdui.org

PART 6

CANINE SCHOLARS, OR
THEIR ALMA MATER'S

CHAPTER 25

TRAINING AT HOME WITH FREEDOM GUIDE DOGS FOR THE BLIND

Janet Ingber

My name is Janet Ingber, and I got my first guide dog in 2006 at age 48, about 12 years after losing most of my vision. I am a wife, mother, music therapist, and freelance writer. I write about technology and how it affects people with visual impairments or how to use a specific technology. Until I was in my mid-thirties, a very well-known ophthalmologist, who specialized in low-vision, kept telling me that I had *retinopathy of prematurity* and that my vision would remain the same. I could read with magnifying glasses, see people, and get around without a cane or dog. When walking with someone, I mostly preferred to hold his or her elbow.

It all changed about the time the same doctor said I needed cataract surgery in my right eye, and my left eye was not providing much vision. The operation was unsuccessful, and I was astonished when a new doctor told me that I do not have ROP, but rather *Leber's Congenital Amaurosis*. My vision loss was a normal progression for some forms of the disease. At present, I have only occasional light perception.

Fortunately, I learned to use a cane when I first discovered that I might be losing more vision. My skills were good, but I did not feel safe with just a cane.

My first doctor said that I could not have both a pet and a guide dog and that I would need to have zero vision before getting a guide dog. Both were not true. I had a 12-year-old pet Golden Retriever when I got my first guide dog, and they got along just fine.

I began my guide dog research by using the internet to check out schools. Since I live in New York City, I was aware of the Guide Dog Foundation, The Seeing Eye, and Guiding Eyes for the Blind. These schools do trainings away from home. My daughter was young and did not want me to go away for three or four weeks. With more research, I found Freedom Guide Dogs for the Blind, based in upstate New York. They do Hometown Training, which means they come to you instead of you going to them. The trainer comes to your home with the dog, and work together in one-on-one training. You both work in your neighborhood and places you frequent. The school uses mostly Labrador Retrievers. I loved the idea. The only downsides were that I wouldn't get the class camaraderie, and there wouldn't be "total immersion."

I had no idea how much my life would change when my first phone call answered by Eric Loori, Freedom's executive director and trainer. We spoke for a long while. Eric asked if I work, and I told him about my two jobs. Eric said he would find the right dog for my music therapy job, but it might take a little longer than usual. He sent me forms for my doctor, and I needed to provide three personal references. When the school received the returned paperwork, we set up a home visit.

The visit went pretty much as I expected. Eric asked my husband how he felt about me getting a guide dog, and fortunately, it was fine with him. Eric said that some spouses don't like the idea.

We walked around the neighborhood with me using a cane. Then came the fun part. Eric took out a guide dog harness and had me hold the handle as if I was walking with a dog. He explained this would help him choose a dog based on my walking style. He told me that training sessions would be approximately three hours per day for ten days. Although it costs thousands of dollars to raise and train a guide dog, Freedom Guide Dogs does not charge the recipient.

About six months later, on May 8, 2006, I had a life-changing experience; Eric came to my house with a large, 2-year-old, black Labrador named Jack. He introduced me to Jack outside the front door because we didn't want to have any territory issues with my pet Golden Retriever. After a few minutes, I brought Jack inside, and the two dogs looked at each other. There was no barking, growling, or aggression. The dogs got along, and Jack respected Abby, my Golden Retriever.

Since I had pet dogs most of my life, I knew about dog care and working with a dog. Eric said that from now on, I should be the only person giving him commands. My daughter and husband were not to interact at all with Jack for the first two weeks, not even look at him. That was difficult since from the beginning because Jack was very friendly.

It was time for our first walk. I was excited and didn't know what to expect, but I trusted Eric. It was different holding Jack's harness compared to when Eric held the harness. I had to put my total trust in this friendly dog. Some of the sidewalks in my neighborhood are uneven, and I tripped a couple of times. Eric showed me the best ways to correct Jack. He added that Jack is very sensitive and will often pout when he gets a leash correction. He stressed the importance of praising Jack enthusiastically when he obeyed commands or walked me around an object on his own.

We walked through the neighborhood, including the broad main street with many stores. We practiced crossing the four-lane street at various intersections. Eric showed me how to line Jack up at the curb and how to make sure I too was in the correct position. I had to learn to trust my dog. I had crossed those same streets with my cane, but it felt so much safer with Jack. He knew to wait for a car to turn, and he brought me straight to the curb each time.

We also did traffic checks, where I told Jack to cross the street when I knew there was a car coming. Jack didn't move. As we walked, I could feel Jack move around obstacles such as trashcans and cars sticking out of driveways. Eric gave me a significant phrase to remember "don't steer the dog!"

While not in training, my job is to keep Jack on his leash at all times in the house. When I went to sleep, I was to put Jack on tie down a very short leash. When I was occupied at home doing something such as cooking, Jack was to be on tie-down.

Jack and I spent the rest of the day getting to know each other. He wagged his tail and rolled over on his back for belly rubs. He played with my Golden Retriever a little since Abby was significantly older, she didn't want to play much.

The next morning, I was surprised to find that my muscles were sore. I must have been tense as I walked with Jack. On the second day, we visited neighborhood stores. We practiced the "follow" command at the drugstore and rode the escalator at the bookstore. Every so often, I get negative comments from strangers about riding the escalator with a dog. Usually, I can restrain my response.

In the evening, Eric came back to my house, and we did a night walk. Jack did great, and I was getting comfortable. I didn't notice any difference in his work during the day or at night. I felt safer with Jack than at any time with my white cane.

For the remainder of the training, Jack and I went to my job, to my favorite shopping mall, rode the bus, and rode the New York City subway. Jack was not distracted by the subway noise, and he wouldn't let me walk too close to the tracks. As we walked around Manhattan, Jack had no problem with the people, the noise, and the many obstacles.

At my job, I do music therapy with adults who have developmental disabilities. I walked Jack around the building, and he was calm and wagged his tail. Wheelchairs weren't a problem, and neither was anything else. Staff and program members quickly loved him.

After my final lesson, Eric told me that if there ever was any problem or question, I should call or send an email.

Usually, it takes from six months to a year for a guide dog team to learn to work together. Jack and I did have some minor issues that were probably mostly my fault. I tripped and fell a few times; I walked into a few things like street signs. We got lost in the age before cell phones with GPS apps.

But later on, I was so excited the day I walked down the street with a Starbucks Frappuccino in one hand and Jack's harness and leash in the other. I would never have done that with a cane. I didn't have to worry when I walked past someone using a lawnmower, and I couldn't hear what was happening around me. I didn't have to worry about crossing the street, falling down the steps, or walking into something. I knew my dog would be watching out and keeping me out of harm's way.

With a dog, I quickly noticed that people were much friendlier to me. They would ask questions and tell me how handsome he is. My husband and daughter have said to me that a considerable number of people smile at Jack and me. Jack is an ice-breaker and has opened up many doors.

Jack and I were a unified team for ten years. We have flown to five countries. He went up to the Eiffel Tower in France, swam in the ocean in Antigua, and walked through the City of David in Israel. The latter involved steep, open steps, uneven terrain, and narrow paths. He handled everything perfectly. We have traveled to many states, including Arizona, Oregon, Georgia, and Tennessee. He has always been fantastic on the airplane, laying quietly at my feet. Jack has attended many Broadway shows, New York Mets games, and concerts. Loud noises, music, and crowds never bother him.

When Jack was about 11-years-old, he started slowing down. It was time to start the emotionally challenging process of getting a new guide dog. I wanted another Freedom Guide Dogs dog. Words cannot express the love and gratitude I have for Jack; he has been my constant companion and given me so much independence. We've been apart a total of one night. Jack still lives with my family and me. He is loved and gets lots of attention. I take him for short walks, and sometimes I take him to work with me for the day.

On March 28, 2016, Eric Loori came to my house with a huge dog named Pete. Pete is a Lollie, Labrador-Smooth Coated Collie cross. He was nearly two years old and 27 inches at the shoulders. I am happy to say that the two dogs get along, and Pete always wants to play. Neither dog has shown any aggression.

Pete is very different from Jack. He doesn't have the exuberance personality of a Labrador, and it took him a while to warm up. He had more work issues than Jack did, but Eric was in constant contact. My husband took videos of Pete and me, walking and crossing streets, and we sent them to Eric. Pete and I became a much better team after a lot of hard work. I had to stop comparing him to Jack - he has a different personality and style. Although it took longer for us to be a good team, it was well worth the effort.

Getting a guide dog was a life-changing experience. It has given me so much more independence and a new sense of security. Hometown Training with Freedom Guide Dogs was most definitely the right choice for me.

In loving memory of Jack who crossed over the rainbow bridge in 2018, and to Pete, my gentle giant.

CHAPTER 26

FINDING PJ

Lauren Adams

In the spring of 2015, I spent 26 days at Guide Dogs of America (GDA), located in Sylmar, California. GDA is where I received my first guide dog, PJ, a beautiful female Golden-Labrador cross. Her puppy-raisers, who I keep in contact with, told me the name stands for perfect joy and that's just what she is.

There were three main reasons I chose GDA: the length of the program, the method of training, and the location. From what I found while researching different schools, programs typically range from two to four weeks. Currently, GDA's program is three weeks, which makes room for an additional class each year. However, during the time I was there, it was four weeks for first-time handlers. Those who returned for successive dogs had the option of leaving after the third week. Some would stay longer if the trainers recommended it. I felt that as a first-time handler, I would be best suited for a four-week program because there was so much to learn, and fortunately, I had the time to commit to it. In terms of training methods, I liked that GDA used verbal praise, not food, as positive reinforcement. I love to give my dog treats, but I don't want her to rely on them for work. Regarding the location, I liked that GDA was close to home. It meant that my family would be able to come to my graduation. Also, I would get the opportunity to work in familiar places during training. I was able to take a tour of the school beforehand, which made me even more confident that GDA was where I wanted to go.

In my class, there were nine students—including myself—and three instructors. The GDA instructors were patient, approachable, and gave constructive feedback. I appreciated the fact that they would tell me what I did well and how I could improve. I also enjoyed the cohesiveness of the group. We provided support to one another, had a lot of laughs, and I made lifelong friends.

Each student had their private room with a provided housekeeping—like a studio apartment—with a private patio to relieve their dog. There was also a snack room. Three delicious meals were prepared for us each day, and they were much appreciated, especially given how busy we were as we learned how to handle all the responsibility that comes with having a guide dog.

A lot of our time was spent learning how to navigate with our dogs through a variety of settings, such as street crossings, restaurants, shopping malls, the grocery store, the pet store, and even the beach. We learned to navigate obstacles such as escalators, elevators, and stairs. Some of us also got to work our dogs in our home area, which was neat. One of the most enjoyable parts for me was walking along a path where we knew there was no wrong way to go.

On our third Sunday at GDA, we had our graduation, which was outdoors under an awning. During the third week of each class, the school holds a Graduation Ceremony to honor the new guide dog teams, the sponsors, puppy-raisers, and everyone who has contributed to the success of the class. Puppies in-training are there, along with some working guide dogs, and the event is open to the public. All nine of us who were in the class shared a little something about our training experiences. The puppy-raisers who fostered our dogs also got to speak. My parents and some of my relatives came, and it was such a good feeling to have them there. Before the ceremony, I got to meet PJ's puppy-raisers, and as to be expected, PJ was excited. I gave her puppy-raisers a GDA travel mug and a card I wrote to thank them for the extraordinary gift of PJ.

I'll never forget the first day I met PJ. There was such a sweet gentleness about her, yet she was full of energy, and I could feel that she had much love to give. I loved her right away, and ever since she came into my room at GDA, I haven't been able to imagine my life without her. She melts my heart the way she puts her paws around me while simultaneously licking me, or when she rests her head on my lap. I love how she excitedly licks my hand when she finds me a seat as if to say, "Look, mommy! Here's an empty seat for you!" She gives me more independence and confidence than I've ever had before. She has such a nice balance of being a hard worker and being playful. I couldn't be more grateful for my amazing dog and my GDA experience overall.

Receiving PJ was one of my greatest joys. More great things have followed in my life, such as graduating with my master's degree in Educational Counseling and getting a job at a community college as an academic counselor. PJ makes going places so much easier by guiding me around obstacles and through crowds, stopping at curbs and stairs, finding objects such as doors and elevators that are in her line of sight, and even finding landmarks such as a mailbox or a sink in a public bathroom. I trained her to locate those two significant objects. She and I work as a team, so we both rely on each other. My responsibility is to know the routes and for me to command her to the right directions. Her job is to pay attention and follow my commands. She has memorized some routes, so before I can tell her to make a turn, she has already made it.

PJ is quite a social magnet. People often start conversations with me by saying how adorable she is or by asking questions about her. It's a great way to break the ice. However, when she has her harness on, she's all business. In these situations, I have to ask people not to pet her or talk to her, because if she thinks she can socialize in her harness, then our safety is compromised. However, when the harness comes off, she's all dog, and some of her favorite things to do are swimming, running, playing ball, and making sure everyone in the room is getting their fair share of love.

This story dedicated to my guide dog PJ, who makes my life better every day; and to Guide Dogs of America, the school that brought us together.

CHAPTER 27

FEDEX, WE'LL GET THERE SAFELY AND ON TIME!

Ka-Yat-Li

When I was 13, I was interested in obtaining a guide dog. When I was 14, I applied for one, and when I was 15, I partnered with one from the Mira Foundation in Quebec, Canada. Now, I am 23 and have been working with a guide dog for eight years. I'm here to share with you my story of success working with a guide dog as a teenager.

The first time I was exposed to guide dogs was when a lady came to my church as a guest speaker with her dog from The Seeing Eye. I was seven at the time and didn't know anything about guide dogs. Sadly, I don't recall her name; otherwise, I would thank her for exposing me to guide dogs. She allowed me to walk around the room with her dog. One of the things I enjoyed was the smoothness of the gait, and the turns as her dog guided me around the room.

The next event was a conversation I had with my friend, Niall, a few years later, when we were attending a summer camp. He had told me that his sister got a guide dog when she was 13. I was naturally skeptical because I knew at that point that most people had to wait until they were 16 to apply to guide dog schools. He informed me that he was not lying but was serious about it. He told me that there is a school that provides guide dogs to children at the age of 11 years and up and that organization is called Mira Foundation. I asked him a lot of questions such as "Are there commands for the dog in French?" "Is there instruction in English?" "What breeds do they use?" and "What are their training methods?" In that conversation, I found out that the dog commands are in French and in English, too. They use two different breeds to cross-breed: Labradors and Berneses (Labernese) to train with the Mira Foundation's students. After the conversation, guide dogs were never far from my mind.

Since Mira Foundation was my definite choice to apply, but I continued to ask additional questions. Inevitably, I asked myself why I wanted a guide dog. Was it to be cool? Was it to feel more socially included? Or was it going to make me more independent? I realized that I didn't care about being cool. I was already blind, which made me different and, therefore, didn't fit the image of a cool kid. Also, I knew that having a dog could be a conversation starter but was concerned that people only wanted to be friends just because of my dog. I desired genuine friendships where they would see me as a person with likes, dislikes, hopes, and dreams, just like everyone else. When I began to date, I wanted a girl who would be interested in me and not because of the dog.

Another thing I was concerned about was my image. What I meant by that was that I didn't want people to see me as competent just because I was using a dog. I wanted them to see that regardless of the mobility aid I used; I could be independent. That led me to tackle the idea that a guide dog would make me more independent as we work together as a team.

Some people believe that once a blind person receives a dog, they immediately feel much freer and more independent. It is simply not true. If they haven't learned how to travel independently with a cane, then a dog will not be much use to them. They need to use their orientation and mobility skill to direct/command their dog efficiently to targeted locations.

If I didn't want a dog for social inclusion, to look cool, or to become instantly super independent, then why did I ultimately decide to get a dog? Kevin, my orientation and mobility instructor (O&M) told me that a dog would guide me around stationary and moving obstacles; including overhangs and elevation changes. I've learned since then that a dog could do so much more, but I already found it appealing because some of those situations seemed more manageable with a dog. For example, I could move through a crowd quicker because it would guide me around groups of people or wherever the dog sees a gap. The dog could alert me of overhangs and guide me around them.

Overhangs are challenging to detect with a cane because they are generally higher such as at head, waist, or shoulder height so the cane would slide under them. It's certainly not the end of the world if you bump into one of those obstacles. You can wear a pair of glasses for overhang obstacles. Or, you can use an electronic aid to locate them, but you would still have to figure out how to navigate around them. Also, once you know where they are the first time, you can avoid them the next time you walk in that area. However, a dog can spot the obstacle and without stopping, smoothly take you around it.

That's why I prefer a dog. It appeared to me at the time that some situations would be easier to handle with a dog. I knew that there were still advantages with a cane, such as still being able to navigate extremely tight spaces independently. One day, Kevin gave me a piece of advice that ultimately helped me to make a decision. He said, "The greatest advantage that you would have as a guide dog user is that you have the advantages of both cane and dog at your disposal."

Once I submitted my application to the Mira Foundation, I was invited to the school for a 3-day evaluation in March of 2009. The evaluation involved assessing my level of vision; the way I traveled on foot. Working with a dog to get a feel for the type of dog I would receive; and discussing the responsibilities of the parent, teacher, guide dog handler, and orientation & mobility (O&M) instructor. The trip was paid for by Mira Foundation, and my O&M instructor accompanied me.

Remember how I discussed the importance of skills? Well, an O&M instructor Mira Foundation partners with, had me perform specific tasks that guide dog handlers need to know how to do. For example, she had me on a quiet street move towards perpendicular traffic and judge where the sidewalk was located. It is helpful to any blind traveler to recover if you veer into a parking lot or if you are walking out of a parking lot and you need to locate the sidewalk. She tested me on whether I was spatially aware of my surroundings. That is by providing a set of instructions using cardinal directions and expecting me to carry them out using a cane.

The other part was meeting a few guide dogs in-training, and I was encouraged to put on a harness and walk with them around the kennel. There is a surrounding sidewalk in the perimeter of the kennel building that has a variety of curbs. It is not just trainers who use it. Students can use it to work with their dog on curbs during their own time. While I met a few dogs, I was fortunate enough to meet my future guide dog named Fedex. When I was walking around with him, the trainer and I noticed that I felt very comfortable with him compared to other dogs. After the evaluation, they gave my O&M instructor and me things that needed to be worked on if chosen for the summer class of 2009.

After the evaluation, until the end of the year, I had intensive O&M lessons twice a week. In July, Mira accepted me into their guide dog class for youths, and I met two of my classmates. Since there were only three students, they condensed the class into three weeks instead of the usual four. The first week, we were evaluated for our dogs and worked on short routes. It included the famous Juno walk used to understand stride length and introduce us to different types of corrections such as verbal, harness, and leash corrections.

The second week, we started doing longer routes which built on the shorter routes we completed the previous week. A long route consists going to the third lighted intersection, to cross it, and make a right turn. From there, to cross three streets, turn left on the third street, walk, two more blocks east and then walk three more blocks north to a restaurant. We were expected to recognize the different types of intersections by their traffic pattern and deal with varying configurations of blocks such as irregularly shaped blocks and problem solve with certain obstacles. Also, during that week, we did a few routes in different environments, such as rural areas and trails.

The third week, we returned to city travel and were expected to complete the routes assigned by ourselves with the instructors following in a car. At the end of each route or assignment, we could get any food or drink if we were at a restaurant and they would generously pay for it. I noticed as I was working more with my dog that my focus on the environment and focus of my dog eventually fit together. At first, I found it challenging to concentrate on both what my dog was doing, and on my environmental surroundings. Instead, I had to rely on more auditory information. One of the instructors they employed was blind and a guide dog user. He sometimes tested dogs for Mira Foundation and helped out during class. Being able to talk to him about his experiences was very helpful.

Although we had time off on Sundays, we were expected to have class on Saturday morning. The trainer usually worked with our dogs and us on how to handle distractions.

Graduation was a simple affair. We reviewed the contract, signed it, and met the foster family that raised our dog. Once I was home, an instructor did a follow-up for a few days to make sure the dog was working well for me in my environment. For example, at that time, I played percussion for my church's worship team, so the trainer was there making sure the dog was comfortable in a loud environment.

As a university student, I have traveled frequently throughout my city and many times to the US. Fedex accompanies me to my university classes and science labs, in a church or learning Krav Maga, a self-defense system from Israel.

Fedex was undoubtedly a factor that contributed to my increased independence, but he was not the sole reason why I became more independent. Some of the credit should go to my teachers and mentors. However, getting a dog has given me opportunities to improve upon my O&M skills and to gain strong self-advocacy tools. Not to mention, my dog has made certain situations less of an inconvenience for me. Most importantly, he has grown up with me and adapted to me as I have grown and will continue to grow into a competent and capable blind person.

CHAPTER 28

MEETING MY JUNO

Ronda Del Boccio

My three days of eternity began before God rolled over in bed at three a.m. on a Sunday morning. Other than the last few essentials, my bags had been packed since Thursday. I was more than ready to meet my Juno. Leader Dogs for the Blind uses that generic name to talk about dogs without distracting them by using an actual name. Since I didn't know mine yet, he or she was Juno to me for now.

During the ninety-minute drive to Springfield-Branson Airport, I wondered for the thousandth time who I would get. Male or female? Black Labrador, yellow Labrador, Golden Retriever, or a Golden-Labrador cross? I was hoping for a hybrid dog just because I wanted to say, "My dog is a GOLDador."

"I hope you get a blond girl," Mom told me for the millionth time.

"Yes, I know you do." I'd trained my first two guides, Thunder and Molly, both girls. Now, instead of selecting my own dog, they would give me one. "I want a dog with a cool name, not something like Andy or Bob." I had seen boring human names like that amongst the graduates.

Leader Dogs provides travel, room and board, dog, leash, harness, and grooming tools free of charge for every student, all without any government funding. My only expenses for this entire adventure were incidentals and bag-check fees.

As I navigated through the airport security to my gate, I thought about how much easier and harder plane travel with a dog is. Easier because of help getting through the crowds and obstacles of the airport. Harder because of tight spaces on airplanes. There's barely enough foot room for a human, and that's where the dog sits. Yet after a couple of dogless years and an ocean of tears, I was ready to have the added challenge of getting a large dog into a small foot space again.

At the end of a long layover in Atlanta, I met one of my fellow students, David. He lived in Atlanta, so he didn't have to endure the almost four-hour layover I did. We talked about how excited we were to get our dogs.

"Did you ask for a specific breed?" I asked.

"No. You?"

"I told them anything but a German Shepherd." My friend is on her second, and no, I don't want any part of that breed. A knot formed in my stomach as I thought of how her possessive, hyper, self-trained alpha service female who had given my poor cat PTSD would treat my sweet Juno.

My travel instructions said that someone from Leader Dogs would meet me at baggage claim. A couple of Lions Club volunteers rounded up four of us who had relatively similar arrival times. We had special tags, so our bags were easy to identify.

I learned how well Leader Dogs was going to take care of me right then and there. I didn't have to stand at the carousel quasi-looking for (mostly feeling for) my suitcase. Then in the van, our helpers handed out lunch sacks.

A couple more students from different areas waited in the van. A tech guy I'll call Orie, an uptight Braille teacher I'll call Fran, who had never been away from her hometown, David and I got acquainted along the ride. Fran's twin sister would receive her second dog as a home delivery while first-timer Fran got hers at the training center. I wish I could have had a home delivery, which meant five days of personal instruction instead of twenty-three days in Michigan, but because I had never had a dog from their school, it wasn't an option for me.

That ninety-minute trip was the fourth conveyance on my thirteen-hour journey, but at long last, we pulled into the Leader Dogs Residence and Training Center in Rochester Hills, Michigan.

I was about to become an inmate, observed nearly every waking minute in a locked campus. We each had to sign in at the desk, get our room assignment and key card. Each key came on a neck strap so we could wear it at all times. If we ever left the grounds without it being part of the program, we had to sign out and back in again upon return.

My room, like any motel, featured a desk, flat screen TV, bathroom, closet, low dresser, chair, nightstand, and bed. They must have thought all their students were giants, though, because I couldn't reach the bed. Maybe it was to discourage the dogs from jumping up since our Junos had never been allowed to go on any furniture their whole lives.

How awful. My Juno will be able to get on furniture at my house. Any dog can learn that some are ok for them to use and some are off limits.

The inside of the closet door had the daily schedule in large print and Braille. First dog relief time at too-early-o'clock. "I am not a morning person. Coming from the Central time zone to the Eastern for training meant everything happened an hour earlier for me.

My Juno won't go out so early once we get back home.

The bathroom had shelves with a dog towel for rain, little Milk-Bone dog treats, a one cup scoop, and a bucket of food. I could hardly wait to feed my Juno for the first time. I found a dog bowl on the dresser with a leash, a Nylabone, and grooming tools. The stiff leather leash would need lots of softening with the oil of my hands before it would be flexible enough for use. That would keep my hands busy while I awaited the guide. I fingered the clasp, wondering again about my Juno.

Will it be social like Molly, or more reserved like Thunder? Will it be a good tracker, able to help me find my way back through confusing areas, like Thunder? Will it be a comfort dog like Molly?

Ever since I found out I was getting a dog, I wondered what toys my Juno would love. Soft? Hard? Plush? Squeaks? Balls? Ropes? Will it have a soft mouth or be a toyminator? Thunder only liked a tennis ball, so she was easy to supply with hours of inexpensive fun. Molly loved all sorts of playthings until she turned two, then she had no use for them.

"I hope my dog loves toys," I said aloud. Yes, I talk to myself.

What breed were they issuing me? Maybe the grooming tools might give me a clue. Golden Retrievers have a longer coat with lots of fringes. They require a rake and a soft brush. Labs have shorter fur, which is much easier to keep pristine. My Juno's bowl contained a comb with no space between the tines, definitely meant for short-haired dogs. My slicker brush bristles were so hard I was afraid of hurting the skin. I brushed along my palm and snatched my sore hand away. I would have to be super careful with the slicker no matter what breed they gave me.

"I guess I should have brought my own tools."

My room had two doors. One led into the hallway, the other to the parking area. Not for cars but for dogs. A strange euphemism for what I called going "side." I never used "out" or "potty" as that's what everyone else says. I later learned that if you spell park with a c at the end and flip it, you get a crass name for the deed in question. This dog relief area had a long strip of pea gravel and a five-foot wall beyond. I explored with my white cane and longed for my Juno. How good it will feel to have that leash in my left hand with my Juno at the other end.

Explorations complete for now; I went into the break room to get a latte. I knew from the materials Leader Dogs sent that they had a lovely machine that dispensed hot beverages, and after over half a day of travel with short sleep, a latte was definitely in order.

"May I help you with anything?" The Residence Assistant asked.

"Yes. Do you have a pole vault pole?"

"Excuse me?"

I gave her a big smile. "I'm too short for my bed. If I can't vault into it, I'll have to throw one leg up onto it and roll in every night."

We both laughed and she helped me get the elixir of life. Now that I knew where to find cups and lids, I was set. Each button had Braille markings. I don't use those little raised dots much, but I can read signs.

The dining room held special excitement that evening: a harness. Hand-made locally, it would empower my Juno to guide me safely through all life's adventures. I studied every inch of it. Jessica, our lead trainer introduced herself to me.

She noticed me fingering the digits etched into the hard leather. "That's your Juno's ID number."

"I want my Juno now," I told her. "Tuesday is a long way off."

She smiled. "I know you do. It will be here faster than you think."

No, it won't. This was day one of my three-day eternity after months of longing for my new guide dog. That soft fur under my hand couldn't come soon enough.

Our first dinner of spaghetti with flavorless marinara left me hoping the food would get better. Each of the giant round tables featured a spinning center on which the staff placed incidentals for that meal. This made it easier to pass items like salad dressing amongst blind and visually impaired people. Slick system.

Strangely, they had no welcome ceremony or opening remarks. Jessica announced that after dinner a volunteer would show us each around and make sure we knew where to find everything in our room. I'm an explorer, willing to wander around without fear, but not everyone is that way. The Lions Club volunteers loved meeting the clients. Lions founded the school over seventy-five years ago, so they have a keen interest. I enjoyed meeting my helper, and I got help finding a few things I hadn't yet located, like the essential pick-up bags.

"Are we getting guide dogs or dinosaurs?" I quipped. This being my third guide dog, I was well familiar with cleaning up the loads. A year's supply awaited my homecoming in Missouri. These doggy doo bags came on a gigantic roll and were as wide as a gallon zipper storage bag but longer. I came across the mega-roll earlier, but I didn't know what it was.

"You'll be glad they're that big," Jessica assured me.

Really? "If my Juno lays a pile the size of this bag, I'll be calling the vet." They wanted us to carry three at all times. I could barely fit them into a pocket without one slipping free.

We all had the same seats for every meal. My table mates included a blond-haired trainer, a couple of orientation and mobility interns and their cane travel clients, and Dawn, who I met online as we commented on Leader Dog's posts. I was glad to have my new friend, but I really wish we had more dog students and less staff.

Ashley introduced herself and said to me and Dawn, "I trained both your Junos."

"What breed did they give me," Dawn asked.

"Can't tell you that, but your Juno snores." She told me, "and your Juno has an amazing work ethic."

"I want my Juno now," I announced, knowing I wouldn't get him or her until Tuesday afternoon.

"You'll have to wait."

Ashley shared a few more tidbits. "Your Juno loves to watch everything, and she wags a lot."

Torture. Pure torture.

After the grand tour and such a long day, I might have fallen into bed if it weren't so tall. I pulled back the covers, swung my left leg up, and rolled aboard. The deliciously comfy mattress welcomed me, but alas, the plastic protective barrier over the mattress made me waken in a sweat. So, every night, I got about three hours of good sleep, got up, washed off, and clambered back in bed to finish off the night fitfully. Do so many clients wet their beds that they need to make us all miserable?

At breakfast the next day, we learned that we would go to the Downtown Center for our Juno training. Lions Club volunteers helped everyone get oriented to the new space, which had various kinds of seating. Booths in one corner. Rounded tables in the center. Bar stools in another corner. Restrooms, vintage airplane seats and waiting room couches near the exit.

Do I really have to wait a whole day and a half to get my dog? Can't we cut to the chase and get through the harness 101 class? I want my Juno now!

Each trainer worked with three or four human-guide teams. One at a time they taught their charges the basics of walking with the dog, leash correction, and proper stance, called the "master position." When my turn came, Ashley told me to take my harness by the handle.

"Are you going to wear it?"

"No. I'm going to hold the top piece in my hand."

"Too bad. I thought maybe the harness was the latest fashion trend in Rochester."

A number of aspects of the way they train struck me as odd, starting with that. I've trained two of my own guides and a dozen varying kinds of service dogs, but I never imagined teaching people how to handle it this way. But it worked fine.

I couldn't believe how she wanted me to walk to a corner and make a right turn. My previous dogs knew that if I said, "right" they should take the next possible turn unless stairs or doors were involved. I could tell by traffic sounds and other cues when I approached a cross street. Ashley told me to walk right up to the curb, praise my Juno (her, this time), then do this special footwork to back up past the grass and make the turn. Weird.

"Is this just for the first few days?"

"No," she said, puzzlement evident in her tone.

Okay, so another thing that would change at home. My Juno will be able to get on the bed and couch, play with whatever toys she wants, and make sensible turns without going out of our way only to backtrack.

We returned to the residence for lunch then downtown to learn how to handle misbehavior and lefts. When not working with our trainer, they encouraged us to practice with our dogs on manners or other skills. I soon realized there would be a lot of downtime with the one-on-one training style.

Since I would be giving mini Milk Bones, I decided I should bring food rewards for Ashley. The first time I praised my Juno Ashley for good work, I popped a piece of cookie in her mouth. She laughed.

Back on the sidewalks, I needed to blow my nose. I instructed my Juno, Ashley, "Halt" and stopped.

"We don't do that."

"Then what's the right word to ask my Juno to stop."

"No command. Just slow your feet."

Weird. "So, we have 'left,' 'right,' 'forward' and 'find,' 'follow,' and that's it?"

"Pretty much."

So, my new car has wheels and steering, but no brakes or power windows. Great. My Juno is going to get a lot of extra training on her. I hadn't thought of it in years, but my friend, Cait said her school dog Paddle came with basics only. I met him with top-shelf skills that she added onto him.

I bet my Juno will learn lots more new skills from me here at school than any others will from their humans.

The footwork-backtrack for a left turn made me think of a dance. All we needed was the music. My shoelace came undone, and this time, I slowed and stopped my feet then bent over to redo the lace.

"Your Juno would be licking your face right now."

"I want to meet my Juno now."

Just before arriving back at the training center, she said, "Your Juno has just seen a huge distraction. She adores kids." She pulled toward them.

"God help me." I corrected the behavior and rolled my eyes.

When Dog Issue Day finally arrived, I could think of nothing else but wanting my dog. People came from some office and talked about something. All I remember was "blah-bla-bla."

I want my dog. I want my dog. I want my dog. I felt like the fictional Bob Wiley in *What about Bob?* repeating, "Baby step to three o'clock." Have I mentioned I want my dog?

At one o'clock, we were to stay in our room and wait for the trainer's knock. Ashley would first tell me my Juno's name, then go get it from the kennel.

Door watch. I played soft music for my Juno and tried to stay calm. I wanted to be first, of course, but I waited, and waited, and waited…Baby step to get my dog. Baby step to get my dog.

Finally, at 2:25, the knock. I opened the door to Ashley.

"Are you ready?" she asked.

"What's your first guess?"

A wry chuckle. "Your dog's name is Jemma."

Clearly female. "What breed?"

"Don't you want to be surprised?"

"Okay, surprise me."

No matter what breed or color, I got a dog with a cool name.

(This story took first place in the Memoir category at the Ozarks Writers League in 2018.
Link:https://www.ozarkswritersleague.com/writing-contest)

I dedicate this story to Leader Dogs for the Blind, especially Lions Club of Kimberling City, Missouri, who sponsored me; Paul and Cathie Tulikangas, who raised my girl for the first few weeks; Jill Vani, her sponsor; and Dick, her puppy-raiser.

CHAPTER 29

WHAT HAVING A GUIDE DOG
MEANS TO ME

Jennifer Bolling

My name is Jennifer Bolling, and I would like to share my earlier life first. After I was born in the 80s, my parents didn't know that I couldn't see nor hear well. When I was about two-and-a-half years old, my doctor diagnosed me that I have *Usher syndrome*, and soon after that, I went to a public school for people with hearing impairments until I was five-years-old. I went to a different public school but was in a classroom with students who were just visually impaired or blind. Being the only student with a hearing impairment, I struggled to learn Braille and made many mistakes, whereas, my teacher mistreated me for that. While I was having a hard time understanding Braille; my parents saw that I wasn't happy there, so they pulled me and put me into the school for children with hearing impairments.

I had someone that came once a week to work Braille lesson with me. When I went to middle school, I went into a classroom for students who had learning disabilities. I NEVER EVER considered myself to have a learning disability.

In 2000-2001, I moved to Wisconsin to live in a group home. I didn't feel it was the right choice for me, but I did it because my parents thought it was best at the time. I had someone come where I lived to work with me on my cooking skill and Braille. She didn't feel the group home was the best place for me because I didn't get the opportunity to work my cooking skill. She said that I did a great job when working with her.

I moved out in 2002-2003 to attend college to learn and focus on my independent living skills. I learned how to cook and clean, reading and writing Braille, technology communication, and Orientation and Mobility (O&M) for cane travel.

I met my husband in 2000 on a voice chat line. We were friends for two years, dated for two years, and then became engaged for two more years! He moved to Wisconsin to be with me. That's how much he loved me!

I was in my early twenties when I started to do some research on guide dog schools. I called different schools and decided to go with the Guide Dog Foundation (GDF). I liked how I was being treated on the phone when I asked questions and how accommodating they were.

In the winter of 2003-2004, I did a required video clip of me demonstrating my mobility skill and sent it off to the Guide Dog Foundation. A few weeks before my school ended for the summer, I received the phone call that would change my life forever. They asked if I could come to their school in June. I remember asking, "This June?" "Yes, this June!" "You mean, next month?" "Yes!" Again, I said, "YES!" with a big smile on my face.

Getting a guide dog didn't just change my life. It changed the lives of others around me, including my fiancée. He was very happy for me; however, it took some time to get used to having a guide dog than to rely on my fiancée to guide me. Once we got used to the new dynamic, he became just as close to my first guide dog as I was.

When I went to the Guide Dog Foundation in 2004, their classes were four weeks long. Today, the classes are for two weeks long, with more one-to-one specialized training time and less downtime.

The school had supportive and caring staff. For instance, they had an incredible chef. He would make sure that there is always something for everyone to eat. You would never leave the table hungry. The staff members eat alongside the trainees. There is a nurse who works the night shift to make sure everyone is healthy and safe.

Your typical day-to-day schedule at the center would be busy with many things to learn and do. Each morning, you get up at 6:00 a.m., you get dressed, and at 6:45-7:00 a.m., you would feed and give water to your dog. Shortly afterward, you take your dog out to use the bathroom. There is always a staff member outside to greet you. At 7:30 a.m., you go to the dining room with your dog to eat breakfast. Someone comes out after everyone is seated in their assigned seats, and announces what breakfast is going to be. While you eat breakfast, the chef announces the lunch and dinner menus. The chef approaches each student and staff to receive their remaining meal orders for that day. When you are eating breakfast, your instructor instructs you on where to meet them at 8:00 a.m.

At around 11:30 a.m., you give your guide dog some water and a bathroom break. Lunch served at noon. You meet your instructor again at 1:00 p.m. to do some more training for the day. At 4:30 p.m., your dog gets more water, their dinner, and another bathroom break. The dinner time occurs at 5:30 p.m. The dog gets one last chance to have water for the day at 6:30 p.m. At 8:30 p.m., you will give your guide dog one last chance to go to the bathroom for the night.

When in training, you cover a variety of street crossings, curbs, and walking without sidewalks. You do some indoor training like in the malls and stores. You and your guide dog must work together as a team with a cart while shopping.

There is an evening where you and your guide dog would walk at night time. I experienced a breakthrough when I took my first guide dog, Jerome, for our first evening walk together. I was walking and telling him where to go; I felt safe knowing where I was walking in the dark and trusting my dog. I felt so empowered, so I decided to do the walk twice that evening.

The scariest experience I had with Jerome was when two pit bulls attacked him at the same time after they came flying out of a window! I initially held onto his leash, but I ended up letting it go because I didn't want to cause more injury to him. I was yelling, "STOP, STOP, STOP!" and "HELP, HELP, SOMEONE HELP!" Over and over again until someone finally came to help. My husband, Michael, was with me at the time. He reflexively jumped in the middle to protect my guide dog. The owners finally came out, but it felt like forever.

Jerome was being loving and caring as he always was and hid his injuries. At the time, we didn't know that he was injured. Once we got home, we saw that he had some puncture wounds. Before we took him to a vet, I called the school to let them know what happened to Jerome. I couldn't keep it together while talking on the phone since I was so heartbroken. Michael had to take the phone and explain what had happened. When we took him to the veterinary clinic, and the veterinarian gave us some medicines for Jerome's pain and a possible infection. Someone who worked at the veterinary clinic brought us home even though we lived just a few blocks away.

Once we got home, we called the police. The police came over and did a police report about what happened to Jerome. The police, instead of us, took the dog owners to court. A few weeks later, we saw the same police officer who did the report when we were riding our bike around the area. He wanted to know how my dog was doing. Jerome was still healing from the attack but was expected to make a full recovery and to resume his work. There are guide dogs who aren't as lucky as Jerome. The two pit bulls were put down for attacking Jerome. To this day, every time I'm out walking, I get jumpy whenever I hear a bark from another dog.

I had Jerome before I got married and had a child. Jerome was at our wedding; I called him, and he came running down the aisle to me! By the time my son, Christopher was born, they both were good friends. I couldn't have asked for a better first guide dog.

I had to retire Jerome in 2013 because he was aging, and he was showing early signs of kidney disease. I went back to the Guide Dog Foundation in 2013 to receive my second guide dog, Aqua. Unfortunately, she didn't work out for us to be a team. I do not blame the school nor myself for what happened. Some dogs just aren't meant to be guide dogs, even with all the expenses and training they go through.

I decided to return her to the school, rather than to work through her issues. I remember when I handed Aqua back to the Guide Dog Foundation after having her for a little over nine months, and that was one of the hardest decisions that I had to make as a guide dog handler. I went to my room, laid on my bed, and cried so hard that my pillow was wet from my tears. I loved Aqua, but my safety came first. When I gave her back to the Guide Dog Foundation, there was a chance that I would be going home without a guide dog.

My instructor introduced me to a black Labrador, and he observed how well we worked together. I loved everything about him; the way he walked slow and how I could get him to walk faster if desired. It was imperative to me because with having a young child, there would be times when I need him to either walk slow or fast.

My instructor wanted to give it a few days to see if we were a suitable match. I knew in my heart that this black Labrador named Dave, was the right match for me, and he would be my third guide dog.

The Guide Dog Foundation do what they call a Celebration Saturday. It's a day where you meet your dog's sponsor, the puppy-raiser, and their family. If your guide dog's raiser isn't able to come to the school, you'd have an opportunity to speak with them on the phone.

Even though I didn't get to meet Jerome or Aqua's puppy-raisers in person, but over the phone; I got to meet Dave's puppy-raiser in person! To meet your guide dog's puppy-raisers in person is something that you will never forget! It can and will be very emotional. I got to hear all about what Dave was like as a puppy!

Another difficult decision I had to make as a guide dog owner; I had to put my third guide dog down. Dave was having trouble breathing one day, and we brought him into the veterinary clinic because we didn't know what was going on. Like Jerome, Dave didn't want you to know that he was hurting, but once we were on our way to the veterinary clinic, he let us know he was hurting. I never let my guide dogs sit on the seat, but Dave did that day. He just laid there, and I just knew something was wrong. I was confused because nothing could have prepared us for the news that we would receive days later.

We went to another veterinary clinic for additional testing. The veterinarian diagnosed Dave's condition: chylothorax.

The vet took three liters of fluid out of his pleural cavity, and before his surgery, they removed an additional three liters of fluid each day! He had surgery on Monday. My husband and I went to see my guide dog, and I have never heard Dave cry before. I know - in my heart - he didn't want us to see him in pain. It just broke my "momma" heart to see him like that.

In his follow-up checkup there was still fluid in his pleural cavity. The veterinarian said that she would remove it, and have it tested, but if this continues, he would have to be euthanized, because there wasn't anything else to help him to live a healthy life.

On October 9, 2016, my little family and I noticed that Dave was having trouble breathing again, and he was walking slower than usual. I called the veterinary clinic to let them know what was going on and that we would be there as soon as we could get a ride. Michael was requesting an Uber ride while I was on the phone with our veterinarian. The Uber driver was so very kind and understanding of Dave's condition.

Dave was taken into the back to see what was going on. We tried to hope for the best, but we knew that it didn't look good at all. The veterinarian came into the room to tell us what we were hoping not to hear. Once again, there was fluid! I went to a corner, covered my eyes, and cried. I couldn't stop the tears. I stomp my foot, again and again, saying, "No, no, this isn't happening!" "Please, tell me that this isn't happening?" Michael, the strong and caring husband that he was, came over to me and just held on to me while I cried. Christopher joined us as well.

We gave Dave as much love as we could give to him in the last couple of days we had with him. We let him have all of his favorite people food with a little of his dog food.

On October 11, 2016, after Christopher came home from school, we went to the veterinary clinic to have Dave euthanized so he wouldn't be in any more pain! I will never forget the last gift that Dave gave me. The veterinarian told us what she was going to do before she did anything. She answered all of our questions.

Now, about that last gift, Dave gave me; the veterinarian gave him the first medicine that needed to sedate him. We tried to get Dave to lie down before the final injected medicine, but he didn't want to. We gently coaxed Dave to lie down for the veterinarian to quickly injected him the medicine. Dave popped right up and nudged me right squarely on the nose, and then his head fell right into Christopher's lap! I had my hand on his body, and I was crying hard. Michael had his arm around me, and the veterinarian had her hand on my arm. I felt movement. I gasp and impulsively said, "He's coming back because he doesn't want to leave me!" I know that may sound silly to most people. The veterinarian was so sweet, kind, and calmly told me that he wasn't coming back, and what I felt was life leaving his body. Meanwhile, Christopher is still sitting there with Dave's head in his lap not knowing what to say, because this was his first time seeing something like this happen.

We prepared Christopher as much as we could about this day, and we left it up to him if he wanted to be in the room with Dave during his euthanasia. He loved Dave with all his heart; he wanted to be there for Dave to the last second of his life.

Oh, yes, about that last gift? The final gift Dave gave me was a nudge on my nose, and if you can remember, I didn't care for dog kisses. I taught Dave how to nudge me with his nose instead of giving me dog kisses during our bonding moments. I will forever cherish that final moment of our nose-nudging bonding!

On December 4, 2017, I went back to GDF to receive my 4th guide dog. GDF matched me with another black Labrador, whose name is Frank. Frank is so different from my other guide dogs. He loves to snuggle and would love on you when you are feeling emotionally down. He is much more sensitive than my other guide dogs were. That is okay with me. I can and will work him through difficult situations with patience and love since all dogs are uniquely different.

When you and your guide dog are ready to head home after the training, GDF generously will give you different items for you both, and here are some examples: leash, harness, gentle leader, dog's collar bells, whistle, harness' light, treat pouch, a bag of food, food scooper, dog bowls, pooper scooper bags, tie-down cord, bone treat, and heartworm and flea package.

Having a guide dog is hard work and isn't for everyone. You must keep up with what you have learned at the school as far as commands and caring for your guide dog.

My advice is to do your research and choose the guide dog school that you feel is the best fit for you, your disability, and your home lifestyle.

If I may share memorable moments from my first three guide dogs, they are:

Jerome: Michael and I were walking by a store on our way to a bus stop, the door opened unexpectedly, and Jerome was startled and jumped, and let out a bark!. Jerome often barks in his puppy dreams, which is so cute!

Aqua: We got a cat named Pumpkin before Christopher was born. One day, Aqua and Pumpkin were playing, and he had his head inside of Aqua's mouth! They were best of friends playing silly cat and dog games. When I first brought Dave and Frank home, Pumpkin was like "Whatever, another dog!" He never played with them as he did with Aqua.

Dave: Christopher has *Autism,* and there are times he will have a hard time with environmental changes and social settings with other children. One day, Christopher, Dave and I were at the mall, and Christopher was upset about something and started to feel his trigger moment. He was on my right side, holding my hand as he was ready to hit the floor with his body. Dave crossed his body in front of me and started to lick Christopher's hand. That calmed Christopher immediately! Usually, I don't let my guide dogs interact with Christopher, but Dave saved the day. I had tears in my eyes as I saw my son receiving help from my guide dog. What a beautiful gesture from Dave!

If you would like to learn more about the Guide Dog Foundation: www.guidedog.org.

CHAPTER 30

ALERT! BEING PARTNERED WITH A HEARING DOG

Jane Schlau

To explain why I decided to become partnered with a hearing dog; it's important to understand just a little about deafness and becoming deafened.

Two hundred years ago, Doctor Samuel Johnson called deafness the "most desperate of human calamities." It is still a desperate calamity. Deafness is not a killer, but it is a destroyer. It destroys so much that is vital in our everyday lives. Relationships within the family, with friends and with co-workers are always under strain when there is a breakdown in easy communication *(Harvington, 1983)*.

I began to lose my hearing around Christmas of 1997 over for a period of three years, I became deaf. Interestingly, I had a degree in deafness rehabilitation and knew some sign. I sought out others with hearing loss online, ultimately meeting many others like myself, and several told me I was prepared to be a deaf person. Nothing could be further from the truth. Having information about hearing loss and knowing some sign language cannot prepare you for the absence of sound and the loss of accessible communication.

Life didn't stop as I lost my hearing – I remember feeling like I wanted to hide under my desk as the world was going around, and I had no idea what was going on. I was an up and coming school administrator and even though not a fluent signer was able to keep my job by working with interpreters. Nothing could ameliorate the trauma of losing one of my senses, though.

Many factors pulled me through, not the least of which is a supportive family. There were also a few friends who stood by me, one of whom was relentless in saying, "Jane, get a dog." I even met several other late-deafened people with hearing dogs. Unable to imagine what a hearing dog would do for me, I learned from these friends that hearing dogs inform you of all that you miss from the environment. How? By alerting you to sound.

So began my curiosity and research into service dogs and in particular, hearing dogs. I looked up many agencies that trained hearing dogs, which involves very sophisticated kinds of training. Some agencies wanted you to raise funds for the dog on your own, upwards of $20,000. Honestly? That was not something I felt I was able to do. Other agencies used rescued dogs. These dogs are fantastic for many people; however, I had a very unpleasant experience with a rescue dog and was hoping to find an agency that breed their own dogs.

Finally, I turned to Canine Companions for Independence (CCI) who bred their own dogs and also allowed us to keep our pet dog. Many agencies want the service dog to be the only dog in the home. We had a beloved pet beagle mix, and we were not willing to give him up. The drawback with CCI was that we'd have to attend two weeks of training in Santa Rosa, California. I learned that it wasn't a drawback as much as it was a gift.

The application process was quite extensive. The first step was an ordinary paper application and documentation of disability; a phone interview, and then an in-person interview. If you get through all that, then you go on a waiting list. At the time, I was thrilled for the long process and the potentially long wait. I was somewhat undecided if getting a hearing dog was right for me.

Ultimately, I learned a lot in the application process and remained on the waiting list for about two years. When I got the call that they had a dog for me, I was just a mix of emotions. Finally, a dog! Finally, a dog? Could I keep up the training? Would I adjust to always having a dog with me? And, of course, the nagging question, do I REALLY NEED a dog?

I informed my employers, now a school for the deaf, who seemed very supportive. I made plans to leave for two weeks of what CCI calls Team Training. All I needed to do was to arrange transportation; CCI offers the option of staying in their dorms. I was a little reluctant at first, but what a great decision all of this turned out to be!

During the flight out to California, we sat next to a person with a service dog. What were the odds? When we made our connecting flight, I noticed another woman with hearing aids getting on the plane. Sure enough, she was in my Team Training class, and we continue to be friends to this day. Arrival at CCI was the beginning of a life-changing two weeks. The dorm was gorgeous and spotlessly clean. You'd never know so many dogs were there. The rooms were also spotless, welcoming, and comfortable. There was a huge kitchen, with huge containers of dog food, and a cupboard for each Team Training participant.

Training started the morning after we arrived. Instructors provided lectures about dog behavior; dog health, and of course, dog training. We practiced training and controlling dogs on the trainers. Yes, they'd get on the floor, and we'd "correct" using their arms or what referred to as "carpet dog". A carpet rolled around this large, well, roll. We learned to be strong, confident pack leaders. A few days into training, we got to meet the dogs. I'm not sure who was more excited, the humans or the dogs. It was like these dogs knew we were their human partners forever.

Pairing with the dogs was an exciting time. We started working with our dogs from then on, both on the CCI campus and out in the community. The trainers practiced everything with us; walking with the dog, climbing steps, using an escalator, going into a store, and eating at a restaurant. The day before "graduation," we as a group practiced all that we learned together, to be sure we'd pass our public certification test. I remember particularly sending my husband out to get a bunch of French

Fries, and we all would throw the fries at our dogs, and the dog could not eat them. If they flinched towards the fries, we had to correct them. And, if God forbid, one of the dogs got a fry, we'd have to remove it from their mouth – and we all did.

We also studied together as there was a written test. All nine of us in this class were in some way connected to education. We were teachers, school administrators, school social workers, or retired from education. We formed an amazing bond. Several of us remain in touch to this day. The day of graduation, we each stood up to say a little something to the crowd. There was a real crowd of volunteers, puppy-raisers, and breeder/caretakers. Each of us proclaimed that we had the best dog, which we all did.

It took time to adjust to always be with a dog as our dogs go with us everywhere. We fly, go to meetings, go to conferences, and vacation together. I remember one time I was interviewing for my last job, an administrator of a school for the deaf. I couldn't decide to bring my dog or not. Stupidly, I decided I'd go without the dog. It was an extensive interview, with a panel of interviewers, then a presentation to the community. The end of the story was that as I was getting ready to leave, one of the interviewers asked me, "Where's your dog?" After this, I never go anywhere without my dog.

There are so many stories; some funny and some ridiculous, but rarely negative experiences. There was one time on a flight on a small plane. The person in the most spacious bulkhead seat wouldn't switch places, so my dog would fit, at the request of the flight attendant. The pilot came out and told her to move, or the plane doesn't. There was the time when another flight attendant, with me looking right at her, mistakenly gave me a braille safety brochure. She learned about hearing dogs pretty quickly. Or the time my boss screamed that she had concerns about my dog being in school. She thought all the deaf people would want dogs. Suffice to say that didn't happen, and the dog stayed.

At Universal Studios, because of the dog, we were always taken to the front of the line. The best though, is a compliment, which often happens when we leave a restaurant, Jannie comes out from under the table, and a staff person exclaims, "I didn't even know there was a dog there!"

All of our dogs from my first Team Training have since passed away; most of us have successor dogs. The loss of our first hearing dogs is indescribable. I was fortunate that my dog. Remick, had the chance to meet her successor, Jannie, and I swear Remy taught Jannie to do a bunch of things that help me. Both dogs alert me with their nose to sounds – microwave, tea kettle, toaster oven, smoke alarm, alarm clock, my special phone, to name just a few. Jannie alerts me any time someone calls my name, which is one of my favorite things that she does. She's learned to get me if one of my grandchildren calls "Grandma!" too.

Do I need a hearing dog? I can't imagine life without one. If there is a commotion in a store or restaurant, Jannie alerts me and points to the noise. If I have my nose in my computer and someone comes to the door, she gets me. If we're out and someone recognizes me and calls me, she alerts me. If my cell phone rings, wherever we are, she will alert me.

We were informed after a while we will bond with our dogs. It is very true. Without explicitly teaching Jannie things like the luggage carousel at the airport or various smoke/fire alarms, or even that people may talk to me and I wouldn't know, she alerts me. Sometimes, she's so good at alerting me to the environment; I get snappy with her. That's on me. She is always right. She hears and knows she needs to let me hear, too. How does she know? She's just remarkable. After all my doubts and hesitations, I can't imagine life without her at my side.

Writer's note: **Alert!** is a KEY work/command for hearing dogs to perform a specific task.

CHAPTER 31

PILOT DOGS GAVE ME
MY FREEDOM

Melvin Reynolds

My name is Melvin Reynolds. I lost my sight in 2003 due to *diabetic retinopathy*, and shortly after that, I received Max, my first guide dog from Pilot Dogs, Inc. I attended Youngstown State University in Ohio, where I received an associate degree in hospitality management with Max, a black Standard Poodle. I am currently working with my third dog from there, a black and tan Doberman named Shamy. I live in Michigan with my partner, Chris. Together with Chris and my dogs, I have traveled across the U.S. and to the Caribbean.

Pilot Dogs, located in Columbus, Ohio, was incorporated in 1950. They started by training German Shepherds for the blind to use as guide dogs. Sixty-seven years later, in addition to German Shepherds, they are now training Labradors, Golden Retrievers, Boxers, Dobermans, Standard Poodles, and Vizslas. Pilot Dogs still does not charge the student for the dog. Some things have not changed at Pilot, while other things have since 1950.

One of the significant changes is that in addition to dog guides, Pilot Dogs now trains hearing dogs. They also have an on-site mobility instructor. In March 2017, they held a grand opening for their new kennel facility that is located just across the street from the school, making their whole operation within a two-block area. The puppy kennel, located on one side of the main school building, and the new kennel for the dogs in-training located on the other. There are some in training methods as well as in more positive reinforcement.

The training time for a new team is four weeks, and the size of the building has grown. Students still stay at the school all day, and all dog-walks leave from the school. Students may spend their downtime in the day room, the courtyard, Alumni Park, or the quiet place where wireless internet is available. The meals are plentiful and delicious for the students. There are two trainers in each small class.

While at the school, students learn things like how to ride with their dogs on a city bus, use elevators and escalators, find curbs and stairs, and how to tell if it is safe to cross streets. Most students will do two walks a day. One walk, taken in the morning after breakfast and obedience, and the second is taken sometimes after lunch. There is also an evening walk and practice in a store. At the end of the training, there is an achievement walk where the trainer walks with the student telling them turn-by-turn where to go. They make sure the students are working the dog correctly and safely before they are allowed to go home with their new guide. If a student needs extra help on a particular issue, the trainers will take the time to work with them to make sure that they feel confident before the student leaves.

I chose Pilot Dogs because I lived only three hours from the school at the time I went there for my first dog. I also picked the school for the simple fact that they trained Standard Poodles. I needed a dog that some of my drivers could be around without worrying about their dog allergies. I was planning to look for a job in the food-service industry where a dog that didn't shed would be a plus.

I had a great time at Pilot for my first four weeks of training. I went back twice for two subsequent dogs, another Poodle and my current dog, a Doberman. I made several good friends during my times at Pilot, and I still keep in touch with them sixteen years later. The staff at Pilot Dogs was very accommodating for someone like me who was newly blind at the time I went for my first dog. They took time to explain things like how to tell if you were at a corner with a stop sign or a stoplight. With the training I received from Pilot Dogs, I have been able to travel with my guides to many places.

I have done extensive traveling with all my guide dogs. With my first dog, Max, I visited 14 states, and with Stryder, my second guide, I visited 19 states. Stryder accompanied me on a 7-day cruise to Alaska. He was able to go on all the shore excursions that I went on, including the one into Canada. Since I received Shamy, my current guide, we have traveled to 11 states. She traveled with me on a 10-day cruise to the Southern Caribbean in March 2018. Max loved to travel and enjoyed camping when I would work for Cub Scout day camps, and he didn't mind staying in a camper or even a tent. I went on several trips as a representative of the Pilot Dogs Alumni Association.

Pilot Dogs Alumni has been active since 1960 and will celebrate their 60th anniversary in 2020 at their annual convention. The Alumni has held a convention every year since first founded. Each year, the convention is held in a different city with a different host. The conventions give members a chance to spend time with other graduates from Pilot while having fun at the same time. Several trainers from Pilot attend as well; and if there are questions from the graduates to assist, or a need to get a new piece of equipment. There are an obstacle course and obedience awards given out. There are also awards for who can tell the best story about their dog. At the convention, funds are raised by the graduates to be donated back to the school to purchase items for student comfort. Members receive a quarterly newsletter and are invited to take part in several different conference calls, a book club, a cooking club and a twice-monthly dog topic related call.

Anyone wanting information about Pilot Dogs: www.pilotdogs.org

I am looking forward to more travel with my current and future dogs. I am looking at starting work as a travel agent in the near future. Our next big trip is to Mt. Rushmore this summer. After that, I hope to visit the other 27 states that I need to reach all 50. My dream trip is a tour of Ireland with my guide dog and my partner.

In loving memory of my guides, Max and Stryder, and with love to my current guide, Shamy.

CHAPTER 32

KRISTIN'S FIDELCO EXPERIENCE
Kristin Miller

I am Kristin Miller, and I'm 27 years old. I live in El Paso, Texas, and currently working with my third guide dog. She is a beautiful black and tan German Shepherd named Eva. We have been a team since May 2015.

From the time I retired my second guide in 2014, I knew I wanted another guide dog. By that time, I had changed my stance on dog breeds. After being matched with a black Labrador for my first dog, and a Golden Retriever-Labrador cross for my second; the bonding and work ethics of those dogs didn't mesh well with my personality. After years of German Shepherd handlers telling me how fantastic their guides were and how different their work and bonding processes were, I finally decided to give the breed a shot. Unfortunately, the school I was with at the time couldn't promise me a German Shepherd for at least two years. There would be another one to two years on top of that because I wanted home training this time. Therefore, I started looking for other options and found the Fidelco Guide Dog Foundation.

From the moment I started talking to other Fidelco handlers and with the school staff, I knew they were the right choice for me. They are the only school that specializes in breeding and training German Shepherds, and they exclusively provide in-home training.

Once I retired my second guide dog in October 2014, I immediately applied to Fidelco. I had all of my paperwork in by the end of October that year, and they scheduled my home interview for November. I was ecstatic. The turnaround time was much faster than I expected. The trainer they sent to me was brilliant and funny. The trainer was wonderful to work with and answered all my questions with total patience.

After the home interview, my file submitted to the selection committee for a review. Since they weren't having a meeting in December, I would have to wait until January before they would review and make the decision. What a wait that was. Come February, I received my acceptance letter in the mail, and I couldn't have been any happier. Once again, the turnaround time had been quick and painless. However, there came the wait to hear if and when they had found a match for me.

German Shepherds are great dogs and hard workers, but they take a particular type of handler. It could take up to a year to find the right match. I prepared myself for that and settled in for the wait.

April arrived, and I got the call I'd been waiting to receive. My trainer was calling me to say that he had found me a match. He was going to give it another week or so to be sure, but he would let me know. The week went by, and then two. I was getting nervous. What happened? Did that dog not work out for me? Did they forget about me? I decided to call and follow up. He then told me that the dog he had initially chosen for me wasn't quite the dog he thought I should have. He told me not to worry because he had found another one that he thought was perfect. We arranged to start training in May. I would have a 12-days of training, and we would train in my home area and around El Paso. We would go over anything and everything that I could think of that I might do with my new partner. The excitement was almost too much to handle, and I think that month was one of the longest months I have ever lived.

The big day of May 19th finally came. I was up bright and early, ready to meet my new pup. When my trainer knocked on my door, I was nearly in tears. He came in with her and had me sit down on my couch. When I was ready, he handed me the leash, and I began to get to know my new furry friend.

Eva was a long, tall and slim slip of a thing but I could tell from the start that she was going to be a spitfire. She didn't warm up to me right away and kept looking back to our trainer, but he ignored her, and the initial meeting went off without a hitch. I receive her harness, and we started our first short walk.

I will admit that that first walk wasn't the swarming butterflies and floating clouds I had been hoping for, but he assured me that it would come. During the entire week, we worked on progressively longer routes, increasing our confidence and abilities. The moment I felt it all click into place, I wanted to cry.

The next week was adding in things and places I hadn't been to before, but they turned out giving us great exposure. We also walked around our mall, through stores where Eva had to weave me in and out of people, and the local Walmart where I do all my grocery shopping. We worked on difficult street crossings I never wanted to do with my last dog or even my cane, but I quickly learned that Eva had the power to guide me across the moon if I wanted her to. Those crossings that used to be so scary for me suddenly it didn't seem so bad. She learned my regular routes quickly and could identify landmarks effortlessly. She also learned to show me the crossing signal poles when she saw them, even if we didn't need them. I was so amazed. I had never had this feeling before with my first two guide dogs. With my Fidelco's trainer, I never felt like I couldn't ask something or that I had to be perfect.

Our last day of training was so bittersweet. I didn't want our trainer to leave. I still had a few doubts. What if something went wrong? What if once he left, Eva didn't want to be this super dog anymore? He assured me that he was confident in our abilities, and we looked like we had been together much longer than two weeks. If I needed any more help, Fidelco would be there for me.

He headed back to Fidelco, and Eva and I headed out to conquer the world! Well, El Paso at least, and I say we have done a pretty good job. She has given me the best confidence I have had in my life. She has guided me through airports, busy shopping malls, gotten me out of sticky situations, and pulled me out of the path of drivers not watching where they were going. She has been there through one of the darkest times of my life, and I can genuinely say that if it weren't for Eva and the bond I have with her, things might have gone very differently for me.

I have worked with and talked to other trainers when things come up, and I have nothing but positive things to say about all of them. The office staff is always there and willing to help and talk with you, no matter the reason. They answer questions happily and with so much understanding. Fidelco isn't just a school where they train dogs. They are a family. I cannot imagine not being a part of my Fidelco family.

Thank you Fidelco, for giving me the independence, freedom, confidence, and ability to walk through life, seeing with perfect vision in everything it has to offer.

CHAPTER 33

MY HERO, ZIGGY

Carrie Ann Mussleman

In July 2014, I was forced to retire since it was the right thing to do as I was well past being legally blind. It was emotional knowing this was an end to my career I had worked so hard to achieve. I wouldn't be able to be a nurse or nursing assistant ever again. I decided to start Orientation and Mobility (O&M) cane training in March.

Due to all my injuries, I immediately knew the cane travel wasn't for me. Feeling every lump, bump, and crack. I cried the day I was supposed to go out in public with Moses, my cane. I named it Moses, as he can part crowds. I felt I would look funny walking in the hospital with a cane. I hated the stares; I felt like a fake. People just don't understand about visually impaired issues. However, the truth was that I needed it. I was down to about 15 degrees vision. I had six to nine months before being blind. To prepare myself, I started a Braille course and continued with O&M until I was a confident cane user. Once I felt satisfied, it was so good to be free again. I had my independence back. I felt unstoppable, even in the dark, going and doing anything. It's a fantastic feeling.

The good outweighs the bad, that's for sure. It's well worth the stares and isolation that my friends and even some family have given me. People tend to avoid things that make them feel uncomfortable, and they simply don't understand. Sometimes it feels like I have a plague. Blindness sure has been a filter. You see who your friends are when you can no longer drive or help them. A family member stated that I embarrassed them while in stores because I had my cane. Yes, people do stare.

I might have lost most of my so-called friends, but were they really my friends? I look at it as pulling a few weeds from my beautiful flower garden. Now, I have gained new friends who are genuinely kind and caring people.

Now that I was retired, I had plenty of time on my hands. It was the hardest part to deal with all of my free time. I decided to make myself a project and research guide dog schools. I wanted to get a guide dog so bad. I narrowed it down to two schools based on my criteria. Accreditation was one of the significant criteria points. I ended up applying for two schools, and I received both of their acceptance letters. All I needed was a doctor's letter filled out, and my orientation and mobility (O&M) instructor fill out another.

I went onto the computer. I asked a million questions to every guide dog user I could find. I looked up the two schools, and there was no comparison, so I decided on Guide Dogs for the Blind. I felt as if I had won the lottery, and I needed this to keep me going.

Guide Dogs for the Blind sent me an information package where it explains the whole process. It also had a DVD to show the campuses and information about it. They provided accommodation like Braille and large print for me. I was doing a happy dance because their program was only two weeks instead of four weeks, which would have been too long for me to be out of my comfort zone.

I was booked to go June 2015, but a month later I received a call that they had a cancellation, and would I like to come earlier for the April class. I said, "Yes, please." They quickly sent me my airline passes and a guide dog luggage tag. They also gave a number to call for assistance and instructions. They would have someone to pick me up at the luggage area. It was official and the time flew.

I had never been on a jet. I arrived at the Vancouver airport, went to the counter and gave them my ticket. I told them I required the assistance, which was incredible because a worker came from Air Canada and brought me right to the stewardess, skipping the checkpoints. She even helped me find my seat and get situated.

When I arrived, a lovely young lady named Katy picked me up, along with another student. She was so kind and drove us to the campus. The staff showed me my room, gave me a tour of the campus and wanted us to get acquainted before matching a dog with me. Their Oregon campus was beautiful in the spring with birds singing, and I even heard a rooster. I had a robin nest with eggs on my secured patio.

I felt very safe because it was a gated campus with trails going around it. We had our private big screen TV, coffee maker, radio, alarm, king-sized bed, recliner, desk, phone, patio, bathroom, and shower. The rooms were all securely locked by swipe cards we had on lanyards. Each night we could dial out in our phones in our private rooms to hear our daily schedule. I loved that. I always have to plan everything.

They were more than accommodating with food and snacks. We had three choices for each meal by a private chef. She was so nice, and I loved her southern accent because she made you feel right at home. She would come in advance to take our orders for the next couple of days. If we didn't like the choices, she would make whatever we wanted. There were vending and pop machines at the end of the hall if you had a late-night munchie attack.

They had a massage therapist there for us, and she was magical. She had the scent of lavender in the room. She introduced me to yoga, which was optional. I thought, "Why not?" I couldn't believe how good the massage made me feel. I almost fell asleep because the lady had such a relaxing voice.

The day after I arrived, they brought me Ziggy. He was 55 pounds, and he is such a sweetie. My heart melted as I fell in love with him, and I knew my life would never be the same. They told me about his history. His parents' names were Inez and Mac. He was raised in Calgary, Alberta with his puppy-raiser.

We traveled daily to either Grisham or Portland to cover our training. I liked the town of Grisham. It is a rural town compared to Portland, which is a big city with bridges and trains everywhere. I'm a country girl now; I will stick to my rivers and mountains. They had a nurse that travel with us each day. We made special trips if we needed anything.

I had a fantastic and patient instructor. Somedays, I felt like I was on Dancing with the Stars with moving turns, formal turns, halt, stop, probe for the curb, then praise your dog. I would look back and laugh at how silly I must have looked. For each instructor, there are two assigned students to take turns. Occasionally, there would be an instructor who would drive in front of us to test our dogs' ability to keep us from harm's way. We knew it would happen, but not when. I was very impressed with Ziggy's training.

They taught me to navigate down eight blocks to a Starbucks. They also had me go inside and then back with a different route. Ziggy made it so easy. I just had to remember where and how many streets there were. I made an acronym to make it easier.

Each evening, we would have a class on care and procedures with our dogs. I found this to be very useful. They would give us guide dog supplies to take home.

We had an interesting outing to the mall. I was set loose. I felt incredible as I went souvenir shopping. A dress from a store's window lured me into a store, and before you knew it, I had no idea how to get out. All the walls were glass, and there was no way to differentiate a glass door from the glass wall. I started to feel an anxiety attack begin. I was about to panic when I told Ziggy, "Find the door." he zipped me around those clothes racks and shelves in the middle of the floor, straight out the door. I was amazed.

Sunday's were our free days. Family or friends could visit, or we could take it easy. We had a pub night on the last Sunday before graduation. It was really fun where we got to know each other a bit better and had good laughs. After returning, we sat and listened to a friend play his guitar outside on a beautiful sunny evening. He was amazing at singing. He sang "Let Her Go!" and it gave me goosebumps.

I had some wonderful people in my class. I didn't realize at the time how genuinely amazing they were. I was impressed, but I had so much to absorb at the time, and it was very overwhelming. I had never been away from home like this as a blind person.

We all graduated from the training program. It was a beautiful and emotional ceremony. The school had our puppy-raisers hand us our dogs. They had so many people in fancy hats and gave us quite the presentation, and it was very organized. So many people had tears in their eyes. It was truly an amazing experience.

Before I packed up to go home the staff made sure my dog had tags, bed, bone, tug toy, comb, grooming tools, brush, fanny pack, wipes, toothbrush, toothpaste, poop bags, coffee mug, treat pouch, clicker, bed, harness, leash, collar, flea and heartworm medication for a year, and a bag of dog food. They also gave me a binder with all his information, including things about him when he was a pup. The binder also contained information about his raiser, all of his veterinarian records, and forms for reimbursement forms as they will pay his veterinary costs for life even after he is retired. It also included photo ID of Ziggy and me together, information on his microchip, and cards and brochures to hand out to people to educate them about guide dogs. It has a graduation class photo with all of us and our instructors. I received my graduation photos and DVD in the mail a few days after I arrived home.

They asked if they could provide anything else, but I would need an extra suitcase as it was. The school had a fun souvenir store on-campus.

I barely slept before heading home. I missed my family and other pets terribly since I had never been away from my home for more than two nights in a row. I was so proud of myself that I had overcome so many obstacles, and there is no stopping me now. With Ziggy at my side, we could accomplish anything. I realize where all the compassionate and genuine people were. They are all at Guide Dogs for the Blind.

I wish to dedicate to the family that stuck by me, and to Guide Dogs for the Blind for being there for me and changing my life forever.

CHAPTER 34

A NEW LIFE FOR ME

Valerie DePaola

There are times throughout our lives that when making a decision and how that decision will literally change your life. I've had many such choices in my life; from getting married, having my four beautiful children, to going to my first Retinitis Pigmentosa (RP) Social, and, subsequently, going to Leader Dogs for the Blind. It was at my first RP Social that I heard about Leader Dogs for the Blind, and my life was forever changed.

I went to Leader Dogs for Orientation and Mobility (O&M) training, and it was a pivotal moment for me because it was there that I got to walk with a guide dog for the first time. It was at that moment that I knew that I needed to do something for myself. I needed and wanted the freedom to be myself once again. It was then that I knew in my heart a guide dog was my next step. I applied to Leader Dogs for a guide dog as soon as I could. The decision to go to a specific school wasn't a hard one for me. I had already been to Leader Dogs. I knew the campus, fell in love with the staff, and liked the idea of a 25-day training program, as this was my first guide dog. I felt like I needed the extra time. Where to apply was a natural choice for me, but as the time grew closer for me to go, I wondered if I was genuinely ready for a guide dog.

Having been accepted into Leader Dogs, I was worried as to whether I had made the right decision in applying for a guide dog, I wondered if I was ready for this big step. Then, I met Roxy. Roxy, a beautiful black Labrador, came into the room excited and prepared to greet me. After meeting her, I knew I was exactly where I needed to be. Roxy and I were perfectly matched, and I knew I had made the right decision to go to Leader Dogs. My time at Leader Dogs was indeed life-changing.

During our training together, the trainers allowed me to work Roxy while being blindfolded. That was one of the most terrifying and liberating experiences in my life. It was then that I knew my partner would keep me safe. I learned to trust her completely, and I was proven right a few days later when she saved me from getting hit by a car. I have been partners with Roxy for five wonderful years. During this time, she has not only saved me from falling down the stairs and getting hit by cars, but she has also saved me in ways I hadn't expected. She gave me my independence, but in the process, she gave me back my sense of self.

Leader Dogs has many different programs ranging O&M training, guide dog training, deafblind guide dog training to a teen summer experience camp. Another program they have implemented is the prison puppy-raising program. This program allows volunteer prisoners in good standing at the prison to become puppy-raisers. Both the puppies and the inmates benefit from this program to learn a lot from each other. I feel fortunate to have a guide dog from the prison program. I believe that being raised in prison gave Roxy the unique opportunity to experience many noises and situations, resulting in her relaxed and calm approach to many cases. Roxy doesn't scare easily, which as a mom of four active girls I appreciate. It allows me to take her to places like Disneyland, areas that are loud and crowded, where she not only works well, she excels. It could be just her personality, but I think a large part of it is due to the environment in which she was puppy-raised. I'm grateful to have a companion I can take to sporting events, fairs, concerts, theme parks, vacation, and my children's schools without having to worry if the noises or crowds will overwhelm or scare her.

Roxy has become an extension of myself, the ever-present loving face on my left. Walking with her guiding me is exhilarating, and I get to use the remaining vision I have to see the world around me instead of wasting it on trying to navigate obstacles. I have my independence back. I can walk around a store by myself once again. I can go for walks, take trips, be separated from loved ones, and go places with my kids alone. I can do all of this because I know Roxy will keep me safe. She is the safety net I need when assessing the safety of my surroundings. When off-duty, Roxy is my silly, loving, and stubborn best friend. She makes my family and I laugh daily. She is quick to share a toy with those she loves, and even quicker to take it back. Roxy's favorite pastime is meeting new people. When meeting new people Roxy wags her tail with such exuberance her entire body moves, and her soulful puppy dog eyes melt the heart of all who meet her. Whether working or off-duty at home playing, she is full of personality. I'm grateful for Leader Dogs and the prison program for giving me a gift that fits perfectly into my life.

I dedicate my story to my family, without their love and support, I never would've had the courage to face having *retinitis pigmentosa* (RP) or embrace the opportunity of regaining my independence.

CHAPTER 35

POODLES CAN BE
GUIDE DOGS, TOO!

Skye Dunfield

I knew I wanted a guide dog when I was 16-years-old. I remember the moment I felt that excitement and wonder deep inside upon realizing there were indeed other methods of getting around as a legally blind person than using a sighted guide or a cane. My teenage brain had a rebellion back in those days, was against anything low-vision related. I hated using my cane, often pretending I could see things others could. I would become extremely embarrassed when I did have to bite the bullet and pull out one of my low-vision devices. Having low vision is hard but trying to deal with it while surrounded by the torrent of emotions that come with adolescence made things worse. That was until I decided I wanted a guide dog.

My acceptance of my visual impairment and the disabled community began when I realized how much a dog would benefit me. Before getting a guide dog, a person must have Orientation & Mobility skills, and suddenly I saw the value in using my cane and other assistive technology. They were steps to helping me get a guide dog. I realized that cane travel wasn't something that made me stick out as much as I had thought and that it was a necessary step to getting a dog. Once I started using my cane, I started bumping into people less often and felt much safer when traveling. I also realized that I could use other low-vision gadgets to help me in my journey towards a dog. Thus, I do equate my acceptance of my vision loss and confidence in myself, at least initially, to the beautiful world of guide dogs and the future it promised me.

The stages of getting a guide were a bit difficult for me for two main reasons. First, being 16 is generally too young to own a service dog, and in my case, I am sure I wasn't mature enough at that point in life. Second, I am also allergic to dog fur, which meant I had a lot of research ahead of me to figure out if it was even possible to get a hypoallergenic dog. I found a few good guide dog schools that trained Boxers, which shed much less than Labradors or German Shepherds, but they were not hypoallergenic. I stumbled across the information that there are Standard Poodle guide dogs. This breed has hair instead of fur and secretes much less dander. Considering they are the best kind to own for allergy sufferers, and that these intelligent and friendly dogs were being trained to lead the blind, too.

Next, I had to search for specific schools, and out of those, it was essential to find a school that used a training philosophy that I prefer. The wait time for a dog was another factor. Standard Poodles are not commonly used as guide dogs because they are challenging to train, and their coats are hard to maintain and expensive. A lot of schools stick to the trade and authentic Labradors and Golden Retrievers. Finally, I found a school that met all my needs, and I decided where I wanted to go: Guide Dogs of the Desert (GDD).

GDD is a small school that graduates approximately 40 working teams each year. They are in Palm Springs, California and breed German Shepherds, Labradors, Golden Retrievers, and Standard Poodles. I applied to this school when I was 20 before I began university, in hopes of getting a dog before post-secondary. The school was gracious enough to get me into a class that started six months after I applied. Even though I had to push starting school for a semester to attend team training, I don't regret it for a second.

I found the GDD class training to be an enjoyable experience. Initially, I was concerned about fitting in because the class size on average is six students, and I was the youngest person in my class by far unless you counted the apprentice trainers. However, it only took a few hours for the comfortable atmosphere to make my fellow blind students and me relax and get to know each other. It wasn't uncommon for all of us to sit together and chat during our free time. We all eat our meals together and listen to our lectures held in the common room. I met some great people while training and keep in contact with many of them still.

I remember "dog day," the day we met our puppies for the first time, particularly well. Students who were attending the school for 'dog retraining' had the option of coming in a week after the start of class. There were only three students when those of us who were first-time handlers received our dogs. As is widespread practice amongst guide dog schools, we didn't know the gender, breed, color, or name of our dogs before being matched. I remember asking the instructor on the phone before coming to GDD if he could tell me anything about my dog. He said, and I quote, "It has four legs, a tail, and maybe an ear or two." I knew I was getting a Poodle because of my allergies, but they enjoyed keeping me in the dark. We all sat around, waited for our instructors to tell us about our matched dogs. It felt like ages before they said to me I was getting a female silver Standard Poodle named Cindi.

My instructor explained that she had a dark-colored head and tail, and a dark-colored strip down her back. Her body was a medium silver color and her legs and face tapered off to a light color. After waiting – admittedly impatiently – for months for this moment, I remember being extremely excited and caught off guard at the same time. I don't know if all handlers do this or not, but I had made the mental image of a big black male Standard Poodle in my head. I wasn't by any means disappointed in getting a silver female; instead, this fake image I had been picturing for months had been swept away in an instant with something new and wonderful.

I'll never forget how excited I felt as I walked back to my room and waited. It didn't take long, thank goodness. I think I was the first one to get my dog. My instructor knocked on my door and asked me to come out to the common room and to bring my leash and collar I had gotten a day or two before. I believe a lot of the staff from the school were standing around, waiting to see us get matched. It must be exceptional for them to see all their time and effort come to fruition when we are put together with our life-changing partners.

I remember sitting down, and the next moment someone brought over this beautiful, soft- fluffy poodle. Cindi was bigger than I had expected, and I remember just putting my hands on her neck and running them down her fur, feeling her and taking in with my hands what I couldn't with my eyes. Cindi was excited and panted and wiggled around before sitting next to my feet. I stroked her back, and suddenly, it struck me. It was my guide dog. It was my partner and my friend for the next large chunk of my life. Multiple people had raised, trained, and cared for this dog, and all their hard work was sitting right in front of me. I had convinced myself I wasn't going to cry, but I may have gotten a little teary-eyed when my instructor congratulated me on my new fluffy friend. Sniffling, I walked back to my room for an hour of bonding time where Cindi and I just sat together and got to know one another. Her obsessive panting died down as she began to relax. Before long, we were in a big pile on the floor, me stroking her head as she leaned in for more affection.

Of course, after our wonderful introduction, Cindi and I got along well for the rest of the class. Because GDD is so small, they offer custom training and routes for the dogs. Before I went to GDD, I had requested that Cindi be comfortable both with being around people in costumes, seeing as I live in Las Vegas where there are lots of people dressed up on the Las Vegas strip, and that she knew how to guide me while hiking. My school didn't disappoint; and during our last week of training, we went to both a casino and a hiking trail. Cindi did a fantastic job and gave me so much comfort and confidence while traveling. Outings that I used to put off or dread suddenly became fun and more akin to an adventure with Cindi by my side. The more time that went by, the more we grew as a team and began to trust one another.

Graduating from the class and having to leave my new friends and instructors was harder than I expected. I was sad to go, and I realized that I didn't have someone behind me as a safety net. It was up to Cindi and me to start living life, so we did. Once I was home, Cindi and I went on lots of long walks together in broad daylight – something I didn't dare do before Cindi - while waiting for my first semester of university to start. Again, our trust in one another grew. Of course, it wasn't all perfect. I don't think anyone with a working service dog would say that everything goes as planned. Some things took time to figure out about Cindi, like how she doesn't like shopping bags close to her face, or her aversion to fireworks. But we learned together, and now, about a year later, I feel like we are over the most challenging adjustment days and have worked well as a team. Trivial things Cindi used to get in trouble for; like getting a little too impatient in crowds and running me into people who have stopped. It's nice when you feel like you have grown together and accomplished even greater independence.

One interesting dynamic of having a guide dog is the various public interactions we have with people in the community who are not visually impaired. I love people, and by the way, Cindi pushes herself into anyone for affection when given the opportunity means my guide dog does too. I try to be kind and patient with people; however, having a non-traditional breed as a guide dog has led to a lot of strange incidences. For example, I take a lot of public transportation. One time, I had just gotten on the public bus and had situated Cindi under my seat when the man across from me piped up.

"You know poodles kill more people than pit bulls," he said.

I just stared at him, momentarily lost for words. I probably shouldn't have graced him with an answer, but I naively tried to salvage the situation.

"Really," I replied, "I have never heard that."

"No, they're vicious. Poodles bite you if you give them a chance."

By this point, I was much regretting my decision to respond to this guy.

"She is a guide dog. They are not allowed to bite," I replied.

"Yours might be okay, but most of them will bite you," he continued.

I sighed, "That's weird, all of the poodles I have met are very nice."

Then the man did something I didn't expect. He reached over, saying, "Look, she is going to bite me" and stuck his hand right in Cindi's face. I was not okay with that and pulled her back.

"Please, don't touch my dog right now, she's working," I said.

By this point, the bus driver had had enough. He asked the man to move to the back of the bus. He refused, as people like this often do, and the two of them ended up in a screaming match. I tried to melt into the bus wall while Cindi sat none the wiser under my seat. For the rest of the ride, we all sat there uncomfortably. It was just that sort of day. There are strange and interesting interactions you have to deal with when owning a dog, but in the end, I think that most people are just kind and curious about what our dogs do.

I love sharing information about guide dogs and helping people understand just how wonderful they are to us. No matter how many uncomfortable public interactions I deal with or reworking that my dog and I have to do, I don't regret the decision of getting her for a second. I hope as I grow older that I will use dogs to get around safely all my life. Cindi means the world to me, and I'll end by saying that she does change my life. I will always be grateful to those who made her who she is today: My partner, my friend, and my guide.

PART 7

A NEW PERSPECTIVE; GAINING INSIGHTS

CHAPTER 36

GUIDE DOG VS WHITE CANE: WHY OR WHY NOT?

The Importance of Accessibility Needs

You're walking down the sidewalk and encounter two people with vision loss.

One person is strutting along tapping his cane side to side in front of him. The other person is walking with a yellow Labrador Retriever holding onto a harness handle. You ask yourself, "Why do some people travel with a white cane and others with a guide dog?"

Is it the places a person travels or a special skill that determines the mobility aid?

If you are thinking about your options or are just curious why some people choose one tool over another, read on to learn about the nuances of cane and guide dog travel.

The very first thing you should know about traveling as a person with vision loss is this: to travel safely and effectively, whether by cane or dog, it takes solid orientation and mobility skills (O&M). The confidence you receive from proper training and practice with a white cane go a long way in how the public perceives you and your ability, not to mention the quality of your safety when traveling independently. You can obtain this training from a certified orientation and mobility specialist.

So, I don't appear to be too prejudiced about the advantages and disadvantages of each tool — I am, after all, a guide dog user — I'll start with the best things about using a cane!

Advantages of Cane Travel

- A cane is easily replaceable and affordable. With a cost between free to $40, you can have a spare on hand in case of emergencies.
- Canes give you tactile information about your environment. You can stop and smell the flowers when you know exactly where the flower box planter is on the sidewalk.
- You can learn your environment faster and more thoroughly. The tactile information you gain from the cane finding fixed landmarks helps you understand the terrain you are exploring and provides concrete objects to ensure your orientation is correct. It is often referred as objects/obstacles detector.

Disadvantages of a White Cane

- Increased interference from the public wanting to assist – kindhearted people always want to help by grabbing your arm, cane or clothing but sometimes their help isn't helpful. (Hint: Always ask first!)
- Cane travel can be more cumbersome and not as fluid. A cane gets stuck in cracks and you get a poke in the stomach – ouch!
- Weather negatively impacts cane travelers. A six-inch or more snowfall with a cane can really wreaks havoc getting around, as it is difficult to tap or sweep the cane and some landmarks may not be available to check your orientation.

Advantages of Guide Dog Travel

- Faster and more graceful travel in general—with a dog you breeze by people and obstacles without much change in pace or direction. They are often referred as obstacles avoider and objects locator.
- A guide dog can be a bridge to the general public opening opportunities for conversation and making new connections. Personally, I have made many new friends

talking "dogs" with my fellow commuters and folks who are interested in learning about guide dogs.

- Guide dogs can be a deterrent to potential personal attacks. While guide dogs are not trained to attack, a thief may think twice before trying to take your purse, wallet or smart phone.

Disadvantages of Guide Dog Travel

- Time and responsibility of daily care for a guide dog – feeding, watering, relieving, grooming and playtime are all a part of a guide dog handler's day.
- Two- to three-week commitment to train with a new guide dog – it may be nice to get away from it all and have your meals prepared and your room cleaned, but it is still time away from work, family and other responsibilities.
- Expenses incurred with a guide dog – big dogs eat lots and vet bills are not inexpensive.
- Dog attacks are increasing and can ruin a dog's confidence and ability to work. With the increase in pet-friendly hotels and apartments, therapy dogs, emotional support dogs and the like; we are running into more and more dogs in our daily travels. Dog encounters can be a dangerous situation with one serious act of aggression ending a dog's working life.
- Dog hair on clothing and in home – lots of grooming and a lint brush and tips for getting dog hair off fabric surfaces is a must.

The Answer to the Burning Question

For most people, whether to choose a cane or a dog is a personal preference. Some of us are not dog lovers and don't want to put in the time necessary for a successful guide dog/handler relationship. Putting your cane in the corner when you arrive home is a pretty attractive notion. However, parting the sea of pedestrians and gliding down the sidewalk with your guide dog is an exhilarating experience. *(Kathy Austin – Second Sense)*

If you have low vision, your lack of depth perception may make it hard to judge changes in the elevation of the ground where you are walking. Other questions to consider: Do you have trouble adjusting to differences in lighting when you go outside or come into a building? Are blind spots in your vision beginning to hamper your safe travel? Maybe it is time to look into training to use the long white cane.

February is Low Vision Awareness Month, and September is Blind Awareness Month. The most important thing is getting where you want to go and regaining control of your life. Choose the tool that gives you the best option for your personality and gives you the confidence to go where you want to go. Whatever you decide, don't put yourself at risk by avoiding lessons from an orientation and mobility specialist on how to compensate for decreased vision.

If you are at a stage in your life where you need to think about a mobility tool, we hope this list helps you sort out some of the issues related to each way of traveling. (*DeAnna Noregia's blog: www.visionaware.org)*

CHAPTER 37

ORIENTATION AND MOBILITY

Leader Dogs for the Blind
Rod Haneline and Erica Ihrke

The Importance of Mobility and Orientation Training

Orientation and Mobility (O&M) training is learning how to use a white cane to effectively know where you are, where you want to go, and the skills to get to your destination. Any given travel environment can provide a wealth of information that can assist a person without a useful vision to safely travel. O&M instruction places focus on using that information to travel independently.

Orientation and Mobility, or O &M, is a profession which focuses on providing individual instruction to people who are blind or visually impaired with safe and effective travel through their environment. This training is available to children and adults of any age. O&M specialists can work for schools, government agencies, or work as private contractors. The Academy for Certification of Vision Rehabilitation and Education Professionals (ACVREP) offers certification for vision rehabilitation professionals.

O&M training before obtaining a guide dog is a crucial ingredient for success. A lot of O&M instruction uses the tactile feedback the cane provides of where a person will step. The cane previews the environment as a person walks, letting them know if there are obstacles, drop offs and texture changes. The cane can be used to locate objectives such as doors, seating, or a variety of objectives where a person travel. A lot of time is spent teaching an individual to focus on cues that can be used by a person who is blind or visually impaired. It allows them to understand their location and how to navigate between familiar locations. O&M training is complex in structure and wide in scope.

During training, skills learned may include:

- Utilizing a human guide,
- Using a white cane,
- Using orientation skills and cardinal directions (i.e., north, south, east, west) to know where you are, where you want to go and how to get there,
- Solving problems along your route, such as barriers, crowds, etc.,
- Crossing streets,
- Re-orientating yourself and
- Shopping, soliciting assistance when needed, and more.

O&M services are commonly sought multiple times through the life of a person who is blind or visually impaired. Some skill sets are specific to certain locations, such as homes, workplaces, and other necessary destinations that are prone to change throughout life. Additionally, the physical changes a person experiences with age, including but not limited to loss of hearing or vision may be a reason for a person to seek additional O&M support.

When a person decides to make use of a guide dog, they should understand that the tactile feedback from the cane will not be present. They will need to rely on understanding the environment by interpreting the sounds and cues present. If a person is applying for a guide dog, there are assessment standards that help to determine an applicant's readiness. The general standards that guide dog organizations certified by the International Guide Dog Federation include that an organization will determine if an applicant:

- Has the motivation to train and work with a guide dog long term.
- Has the ability to achieve and maintain the leadership role in a person/Guide dog relationship.
- Has the physical ability to manage a guide dog.
- Has functional orientation on the routes and to the destinations that they will use.
- Has sufficient work for the guide dog to maintain safe guiding skills.
- Has the level of vision loss that causes dependence on a primary mobility aid.
- Has the capacity to demonstrate independent and safe road crossings (including the use of appropriate assistance).
- Has a safe and supportive home environment.
- Has access to the resources required to maintain the guide dog's ongoing health and temperamental well-being.

Historically, independent travel for individuals who were blind was not widely available before World War II. There was no formal training of specialists in the field of Orientation and Mobility. Few agencies or schools provided more than basic instruction in independent travel for individuals with visual impairments.

During World War II, methods were developed to service the returning veterans. Soldiers who became blind in battle were sent to recuperate at Valley Forge Army General Hospital before entering Avon Old Farms Convalescent Hospital. It was the U.S. Army's former experimental rehabilitation center for blind soldiers in Avon, Connecticut. The Veterans Administration's was very effective at providing effective instruction, which resulted in a surge of interest in independent orientation and mobility for individuals with visual impairments. The first university training program in the area of orientation and mobility started in 1960. The positive performance of the graduate trained instructors and the students who were blind with whom they worked resulted in a growing demand for services and an expanding need for instructors.

Leader Dogs for the Blind realized many years ago that there was a gap in skills for many of our clients wishing to travel with a guide dog. Many clients, without the skills, when applying to our program, needed to travel with a Leader Dog effectively. The decision was made to create a program that took the traditional model and condensed it to the curriculum. A sole intent is to teach the skill sets needed when removing a cane from the process. Use of environmental clues, especially traffic, is stressed. The one-to-one instruction is tailored to each client's capabilities, meeting an individual's needs. Clients spend one week traveling in and around the Leader Dog campus in Rochester, Michigan. The original intent for Leader Dog's O&M program was to help more applicants qualify for a Leader Dog. There became an increasing request for interested individuals to take advantage of O&M training without the ultimate mobility goal of training with a Leader Dog. Clients for the United States and Canada come to Leader Dog with an individualized and very different goal, and approximately 40% do proceed to travel with a Leader Dog.

CHAPTER 38

TIPS FOR GETTING A GUIDE DOG

Janet Ingber

Deciding to get a guide dog is a big step. This dog will be with you 24/7 and dependent on you. You will be responsible for the dog's basic needs, such as feeding, exercise, and veterinary visits. You will need to "pick up" after your dog. When the dog isn't working, he or she is a dog, but when the harness is on, it's all business.

Since it is crucial to be very aware at all times, good mobility skills are necessary even if you have a guide dog. You need to be able to get around if your dog is sick plus you must know where you are at all times, even with a dog. Consider getting a GPS app to specifically geared towards the blind such as Blind Square or Seeing Eye GPS. You can also use Google Maps or Apple Maps on your phone. If you want live help, check out Aira and Be My Eyes.

Dogs need regular veterinary checkups, vaccinations, and additional care if they are sick or injured. Monthly average, including dog food, veterinary care, and supplies can cost upwards to $200-$250. Before getting a dog, you might want to check with local veterinarians to learn the cost of veterinary care and whether they will give any discounts for guide dogs.

Guide dog schools work very hard to find a suitable dog for each handler. They will ask many questions in an interview. Truthful answers will help them pick an appropriate dog. You can certainly let the school know if you have a breed preference, but there are no guarantees. The school might feel a different breed is a better match.

Guide Dog Users, Inc. has published *A Handbook for the Prospective Guide Dog Handler*. Information on the book and print copies are available for purchase: http://www.dldbooks.com/GDUIHandbook/

The book is also available, in a recorded format, from the National Library Service for the Blind and Physically Handicapped. In the future, a braille version will be available, and the book will be on Bookshare.

The GDUI website contains a wealth of information for both current and prospective guide dog users. GDUI's homepage: https://guidedogusersinc.org/

Choosing a School

The International Guide Dog Federation (IGDF) accredits guide dog schools worldwide, including the United States. Their home page: https://www.igdf.org.uk/

To find a school near you, go to https://www.igdf.org.uk/closest-dog-guide-providers/ or NAGDU: https://www.nagdu.org The listing for each school will include contact information and the school's website.

Most guide dog schools provide training at the school; some guide dog schools offer training at home under certain circumstances. In the United States, two schools train exclusively at home: Freedom Guide Dogs for the Blind and the Fidelco Guide Dog Foundation.

The advantage of training at a school is that there are no distractions, plus you will meet fellow guide dog users and several trainers. The schools provide meals and activities and offer assorted room accommodations and amenities. Training programs vary in length.

The advantage of training at home is that the trainer is working just with you and your dog. You will go with your dog and trainer to different places in your community, such as stores, your work, or the gym. You will learn to use public transportation. When not training, you can go about your home life.

No matter which school you choose, know that it will take time for you and your dog to bond and become a team. Make sure you understand all the commands and how to execute them. After you bring the dog home, continue to follow your school's instructions carefully. If you need further instructions or encounter a problem, the school will be glad to assist you.

CHAPTER 39

KNOWING THE HISTORY OF
SERVICE DOGS
Various Articles Compiled

At First, Just for the Blind - (Pawsitivityservicedog)
Guide dogs assist blind and visually impaired people by avoiding obstacles, stopping at curbs and steps, and, negotiating traffic. The harness and U-shaped handle fosters communication between the dog and the blind partner. In this partnership, the human's role is to provide directional commands, while the dog's role is to ensure the team's safety even if this requires disobeying an unsafe command.

Labrador Retriever, Golden Retriever, and German Shepherd dogs and other large breeds are carefully bred, socialized and raised for over one year by volunteers, then trained for four to six months by professional trainers before being placed with their blind and visually impaired handlers.

History:
Guide dog harnesses have only been around a couple of hundred years, but people who are visually impaired have been using dogs for a long time.

The first instance we know about is from way back in 74 CE, during the time of the Roman Empire. A frieze discovered in the ruins of Pompeii that depicts a dog with a blind man.

Archaeologists also discovered a scroll, painted sometime around the year 1250, that depicts a dog guiding a man through a busy street in China.

A medal created by Italian sculptor Leone Leoni in 1561 portrays a dog leading an old blind man with a cane.

In 1780, the Parisian hospital for the blind, Les Quinze-Vingts, started training dogs for people who were blind. Although, we only know this because of "a painting executed by Jean-Baptiste Chardin in 1752 depicting blind inmates of the Quinze-Vingts hospital in Paris guided by dogs". In the years that followed, some hospitals and dog trainers helped patients use dogs, too. So, unofficially, Les Quinze-Vingts was the first school for guide dogs.

Building on the practice of using dogs to help the blind, Dr. Johann Wilhelm Klein wrote a book about harnesses for guide dogs in 1819, "thus introducing an idea which led to the development of the rigid U-shaped harness." However, the idea didn't take off, and no one really used guide dog harnesses for almost 100 more years.

Seeing Eye Horse - (Wikipedia.org)
A guide horse is an alternative mobility option for blind people who do not wish to or cannot use a guide dog. The Guide Horse Foundation, founded in 1999, provides miniature horses as service/assistance animals to blind users living in rural environments. There are several perceived advantages of using a horse rather than a dog. Miniature horses, with an average lifespan of thirty years, live much longer than dogs, and for those allergic to or frightened of dogs, a horse could make a good alternative. However, while a dog can adapt to many different home situations, a horse must live outdoors, requiring shelter and room to move about when not on duty.

History
In 1998, while on a horseback ride in New York City, Janet and Don Burleson of Kittrell, North Carolina, noticed how their horses were able to sense when to cross the street. Janet recalled watching a blind rider compete in horse shows where "the woman gave the horse directions, and it took her around the obstacles and the other horses in the class. It was serving as her guide, and that was

something I'd never forgotten." She wondered if a miniature horse could be trained as a guide animal for the blind. Janet had trained Arabian for 30 years and was familiar with equine behavior. But her urban experience changed her view of the behavior exhibited by one of their pet miniature horses, "Twinkie," on their farm back home. The animal often followed the Burlesons around like a dog and rode in the back of their minivan. From these experiences, they began training miniature horses to be seeing eye horses.

Their first trainee was Twinkie. The Burlesons developed a rigorous training program for miniature horses that was similar to a guide dog. By adding systematic desensitization training, similar to that given horses used for riot control. There were setbacks; the first time they took a miniature horse to the grocery store, it grabbed a Snickers bar off the shelf. The goal was to train these small horses to meet all requirements to become a guide animal for the blind.

One of the first people to use a guide horse was Dan Shaw, and at the age 17, he was diagnosed with *retinitis pigmentosa*, an incurable eye disease that deteriorates vision over time. In 1998, he attended a school for the blind to learn basic skills, such as how to read Braille. However, he stated, "I was shocked at how few options I had." I didn't want to struggle with a white cane, and I couldn't bear having a guide dog because of the grief when my beloved pet dog died ten years before. I knew I'd feel the loss of an animal I had relied on for my independence even more acutely. He heard about the Burlesons' experimental program and was particularly interested when he found out that horses live thirty to forty years. So, he applied to be the first person in the world to use a guide horse. The Burlesons started training "Cuddles" for Shaw. On March 6, 2002, he flew to Raleigh, North Carolina, and met Cuddles for the first time. After some introductory work, Janet Burleson sent Shaw and Cuddles into a crowded store where the aisles were jammed with merchandise, and they successfully navigated the store. Shaw stated, "I was about to become the world's first user of a guide horse. I knew that there would be skeptics—people who didn't believe horses had the right temperament to be service animals. After all, in the 1920s, when Dorothy Eustis began training German Shepherds to lead the blind, many people scoffed at the idea. But I knew that getting my independence back would outweigh any criticism."

Hearing Dogs — (Wikipedia.org)
Hearing Dogs assist deaf and hard of hearing individuals by alerting them to a variety of household sounds such as a door knock or doorbell, alarm clock, oven buzzer, telephone, baby cry, name call or smoke alarm. Dogs are trained to make physical contact and lead their deaf partners to the source of the sound.

History
Hearing Dogs for the Deaf (as it was initially known) was officially launched at Crufts in 1982, as a three-year pilot scheme by Dr. Bruce Fogle and Lady Beatrice Wright.

In 1986, Hearing Dogs was granted full charitable status and bought its first property in Lewknor, Oxfordshire.

In 1992, Anne, Princess Royal became Royal Patron, a title she holds to this day, both for Hearing Dogs and Hearing Link.

In 1994, the Charity opened its northern training centre, and five years later established its southern training centre and offices at The Grange, in Saunderton, Buckinghamshire, UK.

In 1996, the Charity rebranded as Hearing Dogs for Deaf People

Therapy Dog – (Google.com)
A therapy dog is a dog that might be trained to provide affection, comfort, and love to people in several locations. These dogs are defined but not covered or protected under the Federal Housing

Act or Americans with Disabilities Act. They also do not have public access rights with exception to the specific places they are visiting and working. Typically, the dog would be granted permission by individual facilities only. Therapy dogs are subjected to several tests to ensure that they are fit for the job. These tests look at their ability to block out distractions, comfortable around a variety of people with a variety of disabilities and are comfortable and able to walk through many different terrains.

The use of dogs for therapeutic reasons has been demonstrated by many people over the last few centuries, including Florence Nightingale, Sigmund Freud, and Elaine Smith.

Therapy dogs are usually not assistance or service dogs but can be one or both with some organizations. Many organizations provide evaluation and registration for therapy dogs, sometimes with a focus on a particular therapeutic practice such as reading to dogs. Therapy dogs have several benefits ranging from therapeutic and psychological benefits to academic and cognitive benefits.

History
Florence Nightingale pioneered the ideas of Animal Assisted Therapy (AAT). She discovered that patients of different ages living in a psychiatric institution were relieved with anxiety when they were able to spend time with small animals.

Sigmund Freud, an Australian neurologist, believed that dogs could sense certain levels of tension felt by his patients. Freud also used his dog to communicate with his patients. He felt as if his patients were more comfortable talking to his dog at first, and this opened up doors for them to later feel more comfortable talking to him.

The use of therapy can also be attributed to Elaine Smith, a registered nurse. While a chaplain and his dog visited, Smith notices the comfort that this visit brought the patients. In 1976, Smith started a program for training dogs to visit institutions, and the demand for therapy dogs continued to grow.

Psychiatric Service Dogs – (Wikipedia.org)
A psychiatric service dog is a recognized sub-category of service dog trained to assist their handler with a psychiatric disability or a mental disability such as: obsessive-compulsive disorder, post-traumatic stress disorder, schizophrenia, depression, anxiety, and bipolar-disorder.

A psychiatric service dog can assist their handler by providing a safe presence that grounds them; the dog may perhaps lean on the person to provide calming pressure.

Service dog being trained to run over and lie in handler's lap to ground handler on command.

Like all assistance dogs, a psychiatric service dog is individually trained to do work or perform tasks that mitigate their handler's disability. Training to mitigate a psychiatric disability may include providing environmental assessment in such cases as: paranoia or hallucinations), signaling behaviors (such as interrupting repetitive or injurious behaviors), reminding the handler to take medication, retrieving objects, guiding the handler from stressful situations, or acting as a brace if the handler become dizzy. Moreover, the dog can be an extremely useful companion in any controlled training concerning cognitive functions, such as walking the dog.

Psychiatric service dogs may be of any breed or size suitable for public work. The ADA regulations specify that only dogs, or in specific cases, miniature horses, may work as service animals. Many psychiatric service dogs are trained by the person who will become the handler—usually with the help of a professional trainer. Assistance or service dog programs train others. Assistance dog organizations are increasingly recognizing the need for dogs to help individuals with psychiatric disabilities. There are even organizations dedicated specifically to supporting psychiatric service dog handlers.

"In the United States, the Americans with Disabilities Act defines a disability as a physical or mental impairment that substantially limits one or more of the major life activities of such individuals," and, therefore, allows handlers of psychiatric service dogs the same rights and protections afforded to those with other types of service animals, including psychiatric service dogs, are allowed to accompany their handler in any location that is normally accessible to the public regardless of whether health codes or business policies normally would allow a dog to enter, provided the dog behaves properly and does not interfere with normal operations (e.g. barking, biting, defecating, or obstructing other people) or pose a direct threat to the safety of others.

An alternative to a psychiatric service dog is an emotional support animal, these dogs also provide assistance related to a psychological disability but is not required to have any specific training. **These do not qualify as service animals in the United States**, though they do qualify for several exceptions in housing and air travel.

History
Assistant Animals has roots that trace all the way back to the ***ancient Greeks.*** As history would have it, they were the first to use animals, specifically horses, to lift the spirits of the severely ill. Then, in the 1600s, physicians were reported to have been using horses to improve the physical and mental health of their patients. Farm animals were also used in the 1940s by the American Red Cross on a farm where veterans suffering from injury or illness could take care of the animals to further their recovery. Reports show that working with the farm animals helped the veterans put

their minds on something besides war and other associated traumas.

Medieval Belguim:

Pet animals were first used for therapeutic use in medieval Belgium. Interestingly enough, in this Belgian society, humans and animals were rehabilitated together. The animals were used for humans' therapy. Interacting with humans likely providing animals with a companionship that mirrored what they could offer. In reaction to practices such as this, animal therapy became a hot topic in academia. In the 1800s, Florence Nightingale observed that small pets reduced the levels of anxiety and stress in adult and youth psychiatric patients. It began a wave of informal experiments involving animal interaction with humans to produce a calming effect on patients suffering from anxiety. An Austrian Nobel laureate in Physiology and a psychologist were so intrigued by the connection between humans and animals that they developed an idea called the Human-Animal Bond. This theory described how humans need interaction with animals and nature to normalize the busyness of daily life. Dr. Sigmund Freud even used his pet pup in his practice. He believed his dog could tell the most genuine character in a human. The dog would remain close to patients who were free from tension and stress and remain on the other side of the room from those who were not. Freud also used his dog to calm young patients with anxiety.

First Formal Research into Animal-Assisted Therapy

During the 1960s, the first formal research involving animal therapy began. Dr. Boris Levinson found that his dog had a positive effect on mentally impaired young patients. Specifically, he discovered that these patients were more comfortable and likely to socialize with his dog than with other humans. It wasn't until Freud's findings were translated and published years after his death that Levinson's findings were considered valid. This demonstrates the controversy surrounding the topic of formalized animal therapy and makes it even more impressive that today it is so extensive. The noticeable changes in human behavior when interacting with animals is the main reason why AAT has become such an integral part of today's therapeutic practices.

It is probably apparent that pets have a positive effect on the mental health of humans. But can an animal therapy help you outside of clinical therapy? Studies show that owning a pet can help you live a longer, happier, and healthier life. Dogs, specifically, have been shown to reduce the risk of heart disease in their loving owners. Owning a dog or a cat decreased the risk of enduring another heart attack. Additionally, owners were alive for at least a year after the heart attack, regardless of the severity. So, it would seem that animals know the way to our hearts. Pets are also especially helpful to the elderly, who may be struggling with feelings of depression and loneliness. Pets ease aggression presented by those with dementia and Alzheimer's. They also provide the elderly with companionship and someone to take care of, reducing feelings of helplessness that is so common among the sick and the old.

Furthermore, pets are great for teaching children responsibility and reducing a child's risk of allergies and asthma. This is because having a pet around changes the microbiome of a person. It goes to show that even just owning a pet can cause significant positive changes in your overall health and mental well-being.

Autism Service Dog – (Wikipedia.org)
An autism service dog is a service dog trained to assist an autistic person to help them gain independence and the ability to perform activities of daily living. For the most part, these dogs are trained to perform tasks similar to those of service dogs for other sensory processing disorders.

The primary focus of an autism service dog is to protect the safety of the children they work with. Autism service dogs are sometimes trained to prevent children with autism from leaving the house unsupervised. When autism service dogs paired with children, the dog takes commands from the parents, not the child. Autism service dogs also alert parents of dangerous situations regarding the children. Autism service dogs can help open the door for children and keep them from becoming over-stimulated.

Autism service dogs use a command to "ground" their owners by sitting on their feet, applying pressure when the owner is anxious

Some children with autism have been reported to have an increased sense of independence interacting with the autism service dog.

Sometimes there is a child harness that can be attached to an Autism Dog that is worn by the child with autism. Vulnerable adults with high functioning autism are seen wearing this harness attached to the dog.

History
National Service Dogs trained their first autism service dog and placed with a child on the autism spectrum in 1997. Autism is a disability with symptoms that can vary from person to person. Training for autism service dogs is similar to guide dog training. Autism service dog costs between $12,000 and $30,000, and there is a long waiting list for the dogs.

Military Service Dogs – (Wikipedia.org)
In World War I, the Germans and British used brave dogs in various ways to help the war effort; including carrying aid to the wounded in no-man's-land and bringing back the caps of the wounded soldiers so that rescue teams could find them.

"Stubby, the War Dog" was a stray dog who was smuggled by an American onto a troop transport to the European Theater of WWI.

Stubby wound up "serving" with the 102nd Infantry, 26th Division, and it was lucky for them that he did. Stubby not only led medics to wounded soldiers, but he also alerted his comrades when a German spy tried to sneak past the ranks. After the war, Stubby met with U.S. presidents, marched in American Legion parades, and received honors from the Red Cross and the Humane Society.

With war comes wounds, and dogs helped veterans (and others) after World War 1. Germany pioneered the use of dogs to help guide veterans who were blind. By 1927, an estimated 4,000 Germans were using guide dogs!

After World War One, Germany issued these stamps in honor of the Oldenberg school for training guide dogs. Some of the stamps use the word, "Fuhrer," but in this context, the word does not refer to Adolph Hitler, but instead, it just means the word "leader". Thus, one of the stamps has the translation (very roughly) translates as "He leads him from sidewalk to sidewalk".

From Germany to the USA- Wider Range in Service Dogs Training

Miriam Ascarelli, in her book, *Independence Vision: Dorothy Harrison Eustis and the Story of the Seeing Eye*, tells the following inspiring story: In 1923, an American woman, Dorothy Harrison Eustis, started breeding and training German Shepherds in nearby Switzerland to work as police and military dogs. Four years later, she wrote a story about the guide dogs in Germany for *The Saturday Evening Post*. Morris Frank, an American who was blind, wrote to her and asked, "Is what you say really true? If so, I want one of those dogs! And, I am not alone. Thousands of blind like me abhor being dependent on others. Help me, and I will help them. Train me, and I will bring back my dog and show people here how a blind man can be absolutely on his own. We can then set up an instruction center in this country to give all those here who want it a chance at a new life." Ms. Eustis trained a guide dog for Mr. Morris, who traveled to Switzerland. He partnered with the dog; a female German Shepherd named Kiss—whom he promptly renamed Buddy (the same name as the next six guide dogs he owned). Eustis later founded the first guide-dog training school in the United States, and in the following years, schools and organizations were established all over Europe.

In the 1930s, the Swiss Army began training dogs for avalanche and snow rescue, and in World War II, all sides of the conflict started training dogs for military work.

Thus, when US soldiers came back from World War II, some of them were experienced dog trainers. Some of these ex-servicemen started teaching classes for civilian dog owners.

In the 1970s, studies of puppy development revealed the importance of early socialization for puppies. It is challenging to work with rescue dogs if they lack early socialization. When poorly socialized puppies grow into adult dogs, the best of training can't make up for their developmental deficiencies. By then the dogs are way past the "window of socialization" that is available only during puppyhood. While we rescue adult dogs, this fact does complicate their selection. We must be extra careful to test to see that an adult dog received proper socialization as a puppy.

In 1990, the Americans with Disabilities Act (ADA) passed its law, and it defined the idea that service dogs could be used to help with conditions other than blindness and deafness.

Originally, the ADA stated that service animals could be any species, so people in wheelchairs sometimes used monkeys for picking up dropped objects and such. The Americans with Disabilities Act has since tightened their regulations, and the law now states that "only dogs can qualify as service animals. (In a few special cases, miniature horses also qualify)" As the service dog industry continued to grow, organizations were formed to help certify both service dog training organizations and service dogs.

Around the 1990s and the 2000s, people started training service dogs to help with a broader range of disabilities. Various species of dogs were trained to assist children and adults with autism, people with diabetes, and veterans. They also assisted others who have PTSD, people with other emotional and psychological disorders, and many others.

CHAPTER 40

UNDERSTANDING SERVICE DOGS' ROLES
Various Articles Compiled

Misconceptions and Clarifications - (ADA.gov)
Service dogs provide invaluable assistance to their handlers. These unique working animals undergo extensive and highly specialized training to learn how to mitigate the difficulties caused by specific disabilities

"When you have a service animal, it's like you are one. When I put my hand on his harness - it's like an extension of my arm - that's putting a value on your freedom. How do you say what your freedom is worth? It's worth everything."

Under the Americans with Disabilities Act (ADA), service dogs and their handlers are afforded numerous rights.

How the ADA Defines a Disability
ADA Service Dog Laws prohibit discrimination against disabled people with service animals in employment, public accommodations, state and local government activities, public transportation, commercial facilities, and telecommunication.

What Is a Service Animal?
The ADA also has a strict definition of service animals. By definition, these They "dogs that are individually trained to do work or perform tasks for people living with disabilities".

Service dogs are working animals – **not pets.** They must be trained to perform a task that is directly related to the handler's disability. The ADA does not recognize dogs who solely provide emotional support or comfort as service animals.

- Service Animals: Trained to perform tasks for disabled handlers
- Facility/Therapy Animals: Trained to provide affection, comfort, and love to people
- Comfort/Companion: Provide emotional support only

Where Service Dogs Are Allowed:
Businesses, nonprofit organizations, and state and local governments are required to allow service dogs, under the service dog laws, to accompany people with disabilities in public places. They must be allowed in establishments that prepare or serve food regardless of local or state health codes prohibiting animals on the premises. **ADA service dog laws will always overrule local laws.**

People with disabilities and their services are not to be isolated from other customers or patrons. They also may not be treated less favorably or be required to pay additional fees for their animals. Businesses that charge additional fees or deposits for pets – such as hotels – must waive these fees for service animals. (You can be charged if damages caused by your service dogs – See Ada.gov)

- Service Animals: Access rights in all public places with some exceptions: Religion institutions, private institutions, and sterile environments.
- Facility/Therapy Animals: Approved by hospitals, schools, courthouses, disaster areas, etc.
- Emotional/Support/Companion Animals: No public or private access rights. Fair Housing Act Protection and Air Carrier Access Act provide access for people with emotional/anxiety needs. Psychiatrics' written note is required.

Requirements for Service Dog and Handler Teams:
Under the ADA, all service dogs must be leashed, harnessed, or tethered. If, however, these devices interfere with the dog's work

or the handler's disability makes it impossible to use them, the dog may be kept under control through voice, signal, or other controls.

If a service dog is not under control and the handler fails to act to gain to control, a business owner or staff member is permitted to ask that the animal be removed from the premises. A handler may also be asked to remove a service dog that is not housebroken, is behaving aggressively, or is otherwise posing a threat to human health and safety. If the dog must be removed for a legitimate reason, the establishment must permit the handler to obtain the services or goods they need without the animal's presence. (See Appendix A: ADA for more detailed information)

The Rise in "Fake" Service Dogs – (Thewholepetvet.com)
Service dogs who provide mental, emotional or physical support have made it possible for people with disabilities to live independently. Currently, there are businesses' websites advertising a bogus certification and/or registration for support animals. **(Registration or certification is NOT required or recognized by the ADA. Reputable training facilities can certify their highly-trained service dogs went through an intense training process and graduated with its handler).**

"There's No Such Thing!"
According to the Americans with Disabilities Act (ADA), there is no uniform nationwide certification or registration process for legitimate service animals. These animals receive up to several years of specialized training – making it easy for people to scam a non-existent system. Also, the easy availability online of 'service dog' harnesses and vests are all too tempting for animal-owners who want company running errands and going out.

Where there is a service, privilege or right, especially when it comes to animals, it seems there are always people willing to bend the rules / circumvent the systems. It usually involves money when selling their so-called "service dog certification" to designate animals with qualifications that they don't have. The types of service and support animals are vast and can be confusing.

We are so lucky in this society to have this term of emotional support animal and we really should designate that of the people who need them but when people are taking advantage of the system that is really hard, it's disappointing.

The American with Disabilities Act (ADA) says support animals do not have the same federal protections as service animals. Business owners may ask someone with a disability only two questions regarding their service animal.

It's often obvious when an animal is a bona-fide service dog, such as when they are guiding someone who is unable to see, is in a wheelchair or has trouble with stability or balance, but other times, disabilities aren't evident.

Fees – (R.Rice)

Service animals must be under the control of their person **AT ALL TIMES** in order to be allowed to accompany their person into any establishment. It means, according to most/all hotels that service animals cannot be left alone in a hotel room when their disabled person leaves (what's the point for a service dog waiver if your 'service' dog is not with you as needed?). The dogs are not granted to swim in public pools, seated in the restaurant's chair or on a table, etc.

- Hotels: No deposits or cleaning fees allowed **UNLESS** the service animals cause damages.
- Airlines: No pets or cargo fees. If your service dog is too large you may be asked to purchase another seat or to place your dog in cargo.

- City Animal Control: May waive yearly's license tag but not required.
- Housing: No ESA pet/service animals' deposit or monthly's fees are allowed.

Support our Business Retailers – (R.Rice & NBC News5)
Recently, nearly two dozen states have tightened the leash recently on pet owners for illegitimately passing off their pets as service animals. Those who misrepresent their dog feel they can bring them into restaurants, theaters, grocery stores, and other public places.

Many states are now passing legislation bills to fine and charge a misdemeanor to pet owners who fraudulently representing their pets as service animals. *(See below posts from news / social media)*

"I couldn't go into a store, or an airport, or even an office without seeing some disorderly four-legged creature dragging its owner around, wearing a vest that said, "service animal."
Arizona State Senate, John Kavanagh, AZ Central and NBC News5

"I would see people in the supermarkets with animals in the shopping cart or walking around sniffing the food."
Anonymous, NY

"Business owners and restaurants don't want to delve into whether the animal is a "service" animal – protected under the ADA or a "support" pet out of fear of being sued. Support animals are not protected under the ADA, with exceptions for those comfort veterans suffering from Post-Traumatic Stress Disorder."
Exec Dir, National Disability Rights Network, Curt Decker, NBC News5

"It's compounded by the confusing terminology" People prey upon that with the purpose of gaming the system".
National Dir of Research and Therapy Programs at American Humane, Amy McCullough, NBC News5

"Just because one person felt the rules don't apply to them. This leads businesses to pressure legislators against ADA rules, which only ends up hurting the people it was created to protect."
Guide Dog for the Blind Puppy Raiser, Anonymous

"Your untrained emotional support dog just stole something valuable from a young boy. I am so upset at you."
Elise Lalor, FB poster

"I can't say why somebody else feels that you could just get a vest and put it on a dog. That's not what makes it a service dog."
Patrick Branam, father of a son with autism, Bryson, Kentucky, Mountain News (WYMT)

"It's becoming a problem; I've heard a lot from service animal owners that the people with emotional support animals are kind of damaging their brand. More and more people are saying, 'I qualify for an emotional support animal, you need to rent housing to me,' when they do not."
Jim Dunnigan, Utah House Representative, Fox13

"Mental health professionals are supposed to evaluate patients before declaring them in-need of an emotional support animal. Our investigation found one doctor willing to bypass that process for a fee."
NBC News 5 Investigator, Eric Ross

"I would like to have my eyes back and not have a dog. People with disabilities really need these dogs to make life more accessible and mobile for us."
Councilwoman, Yolanda Avila, NBC News5

The issue of fake service dogs/animals transcends retail businesses and housing management. It has become such a problem where several states are now passing their own laws to combat this issue. Click on this website link below to see the states that have passed "fake service dog/animal" laws. It offers a brief overview of what the penalty is, and where you can find more information on that states law: www.propertyware.com

CHAPTER 41

FREEDOM FIDOS' MISSION

R.Rice

Aa Columbus, Georgia based non-profit organization, Freedom Fidos trained shelter dogs to be task-trained service dogs for heroes at no cost to the recipient.

Matt Burgess spent eight years in the US Army with deployments to Iraq, Bosnia, and Macedonia. During those deployments, he experienced four blast explosions resulting in traumatic brain injury, as well as a reaction to the Anthrax Vaccination. It caused him to face eighteen medical conditions which forced him into early retirement in 2007.

Matt found his passion by serving to the populations of veterans and first responders with many dog teams while there are over 200 applicants on a waiting list to start their training. Freedom Fidos' service dogs have repeatedly provided hope, often where there are none. The healing they provide is often indescribable, beyond comprehension, yet so visible.

What is Freedom Fidos?

Freedom Fidos' rescues dogs (the majority) from high-risk kill shelters, task trains them and places them with our veterans and first responders.

Freedom Fidos trains the dog to meet the specific needs of the individual. Freedom Fidos trains the service dog to meet the needs of individuals with physical disabilities. We know if an individual experiences *PTSD*, and the service dog will also be instrumental in that area as well. We believe there are adequate service dog organizations to serve; while our niche is traumatic brain injury and physical disabilities. This makes compliance with the ADA more feasible and demonstrable.

When the Freedom Fidos trainers, Matt Burgess and Kristine Duncan, go to a shelter, they walk through the shelter bouncing a tennis ball. While all of the dogs watch the tennis ball bouncing 20 minutes later, then it is most likely the "drivey" canines. Then, they will be chosen in learning the required task. Tennis Ball training is one of Matt's favorite training techniques. Freedom Fidos' training techniques could best be described by searching for what motivates the individual canine. Usually, it is a mix of praise, touch, connection, treats, toys, tennis balls, as well as often very cerebral and or drivey canines, like Brinks (Matt's service dog), who are intensely focused until they learn a task. Freedom Fidos often uses the verbiage from *The Five Love Languages* book to describe a more focused motivational behavior the canine exhibits. Brinks is, primarily, acts of service.

Freedom Fidos also incorporates taking Brinks with Matt and Kristine to a shelter to select a potential service-dog-in-training (SDIT). While Matt and Kristine try, often known to put dog bones in their mouth and hand it to the canine, they still don't speak "Doganese" as Brinks does. Brinks can sense something which might not be visible to Matt and Kristine. They have learned to trust Brinks and allow him to be the ultimate authority.

Freedom Fidos, comprised of all volunteers and 25 board members, they have created 50 service dog-teams since their inception and have 200 plus applicants on their waiting list. Currently, they have two volunteers who maintain daily facility activities.

Due to their incredible growth - Freedom Fidos' Board of Directors will create salaried secretary and dog trainer positions so they can sufficiently meet the needs of veteran and first responder populations.

While working with Freedom Fidos, these people discover and embrace their inner strength to overcome harsh obstacles and adversity in their quest for acceptance, equality, and respect by society. Even the simplest everyday tasks people take for granted, such as public transportation, cooking, or even walking around can be a Herculean challenge for those with a disability. They keep on fighting and adapting to those constant challenges. These people, along with their families and friends, are unseen and unheard heroes.

Freedom Fidos Service Dog Handlers' Testimonies~

"The day I received Junior from Freedom Fidos I was able to stop taking three psychotropic medications the VA has prescribed to me. I have stayed off of those medications for the last two months, and I swear it's like Junior has been able to heal things which no other resource could heal. For the past two months, I have traveled to 30 state parks and interacted with numerous people. I don't know if I would have been able to do this if I didn't have Junior. Every morning, I wake up to his panting, tongue licking my face.

In contrast to many days when I would have stayed in bed before, I now am excited to start my day with my best friend. He is my little healer, best friend, and gives me so many other things which I can't even describe. Thank you for saving my life, Freedom Fidos!"
Hampton Sceron

"My name is Carl Colarusso. I've retired Army with 25 years of service. I have PTSD in addition to numerous other health problems. Recently, the Army sent my son home with an honorable discharge because he was ill. He cut his head in a blast which never healed. So, I moved my son to my home in South Carolina. Our VA here in Myrtle Beach also diagnosed him with PTSD. They did a chest MRI and swore that nothing was wrong. I was a medic 25 years and a 91 C medical specialist; therefore, I could see the fluid sacks around his heart, kidneys, and liver. When my son passed away soon after, it sent me in a downward spiral. I was just waiting to die.

But one evening my wife (Beth) and I were watching the local news, and a short clip about Freedom Fidos was on. I called the phone number that they gave. It was the call that changed my life forever. I had been trying to get a service dog from different agencies for 18 years. The going price was six thousand dollars or more. Other organizations wanted me to come to their location to help them raise funds, which were not a possibility due to my medical conditions. However, Freedom Fidos came to my house and was true to their advertising, which stated it was free. Matt Burgess, founder/lead trainer and a disabled veteran himself, came to my home. We spoke, and he evaluated my Chesapeake Bay Retriever. We worked until Gunner was nine months old. During this process, Matt also took Gunner into his own pack to continue Gunner's training. I now feel good about myself and those around me.

We are honored to be able to tell you that due to our experience with Freedom Fidos and Mr. Matt Burgess, that our 7-month old Chesapeake Bay Retriever has been transformed from a puppy to a dog of dignified stature. Our dog, Gunner, is now a working companion to help keep me calm and centered. I suffer from many back problems and am listed as 100% PTSD from the VA.

I feel that I have a new lease on life. Everywhere we go, from doctor offices to grocery stores or group therapy at the VA, Freedom Fidos and Matt are on our lips. We can't tell enough people how Matt has transformed our lives. Gunner does all that he is asked or expected of him and more. Whether it be walking with my wife Beth around the neighborhood or assisting to my needs and providing aid and comfort to me when I am stressed, receive numerous benefits from Gunner.

My health has dramatically improved, including weight loss, lower blood pressure, and lower blood sugar levels from my time spent with Gunner. We want to thank Freedom Fidos and Matt for still serving those of us who served our country." God Bless America!
Carl and Beth Colarusso, U.S. Army Ret.

"Wow, I am so happy and excited to find Freedom Fidos. I have been trying for one and half years to get my dog, Jethro, trained to be my service dog. Many organizations wanted to give me one of their dogs but wouldn't train my dog. The ones that would train Jethro wanted $4000-

$8000 even though they said it was free to veterans. Freedom Fidos is a "NO BS", no fee for veterans. He trains Jethro two to three times a week with great improvement. I had been paying $60 an hour to a previous trainer and would only get lessons twice a month. Frequently, I waited over two months. Matt is always on time and willing to be flexible with my schedule needs. I would give this "REAL" non-profit 10 star's if I could. I can't find enough words to express how pleased I am."
Craig Watford

"Although, I received some positive results at two other service dog organizations before I found this organization, Freedom Fidos. Matt understood me and my needs not only as a service dog handler but also as a veteran. When I informed him, I was receiving a heart catheter; he would have been on his way to the hospital immediately if I had allowed him. He taught my dog, Croghan, things that no one else had been able to do. Other organizations taught me what to do as a service dog handler. Matt taught me how to think, which has resulted in me getting positive feedback about Croghan every time I am in public. During a recent three day stay in the hospital, Croghan behaved so well that he became the nurse's favorite, leaving me a little envious. Matt and Freedom Fidos has become like family to me."
Boot Sessoms

"A special thanks to Matt Burgess for providing this wonderful dog named Bronson to our son, Austin. Matt was able to rescue Bronson from an abusive owner where he suffered much physical and emotional abuse. Austin likewise endured difficult first several years of his life where he was the victim of both physical and emotional abuse. He was removed from that abusive home life and placed with our family. We adopted Austin was into our family, along with his sister Trinity. Matt, with his keen sense of understanding dogs, was able to see an instant connection between the two. He was very gracious in providing Bronson to Austin. The two have become simply inseparable. They have impacted each other's life most remarkably.. Austin has multiple orthopedic issues that will need medical intervention in the near future as well as ongoing emotional support. The improvement we have seen in Austin since Bronson entered his life is just amazing. An old poet once said that a dog could somehow sense the innermost workings of the human heart. They

both seem to understand the travails the other has endured. Their bond and connection have succeeded in all of our expectations. Thanks again, Matt, for your graciousness, your service to our country, and most of all, your friendship." God Bless!
The Shenyos

Freedom Fidos Logo

The name Freedom Fidos is not just patriotic; it comes from the sincere desire to provide a service dog that gives a disabled veteran the freedom to live their life and pursue a new more hopeful future.

The shield represents the support that the veteran receives from Freedom Fidos, while also representing the protection that their service dog will provide them from all kinds of situations.

The three stars were strategically chosen to represent hope, light, and love. Reminding the Wounded Warrior each time they look at this patch that the sky is the limit.

The dog holding the flag is Brinks, Matt's service dog. Brinks inspired Matt to continue to climb in life but also gave him purpose. Since Brinks was the one to inspire this path, it is fitting he inspires all the future disabled veterans as well. Brinks earned the title, "Canine-Co Founder".

The colors, chosen for the logo are based on Eastern philosophies, in the hopes that they provide and promote a sense of healing and hope. Freedom Fidos' service dogs have repeatedly provided hope, often where there was none. The healing they provide is often indescribable, beyond comprehension, yet so visible.

Freedom Fidos firmly believes and has watched natures ultimate healers restore humanity, which is often lost or diminished during the war as well as any traumatic event. Because the balance is the natural order when they are in nature or the pack structure. They sense when their handler is out of balance, whether physically or emotionally, and seek to restore that balance.

Brinks holding the flag stems from an actual photo during which Brinks held the flag cheerfully for five minutes. He did so from a standard canine desire to please and connect with Matt. Consequently, the photo, leading to the embroidered patch, is to provide hope and assurance to all Freedom Fidos' future service dog handlers. Your canine will do the same through their incredible ability to connect. Their training received at Freedom Fidos combined with the indescribable connection and bond which will form once placed with their handler that will create a powerful and impactful journey.

Service Dogs for Veterans
Awareness Week Proclamation

An official announcement of great importance: Governor Kemp signed a proclamation to show support for all veterans in need for a service dog in public places. The State of Georgia is committed to providing all possible assistance to its many accomplished and respected veterans who become disabled through their services to our nation.

Georgia is the first state to have such proclamation called "Service Dogs for Veterans Awareness Week." It is appropriate to celebrate the achievements of veterans who are disabled and further raise awareness of their needs between October 6th and 12th annually. Freedom Fidos' goal is to empower wounded heroes to live healthily and independently with the help of task-trained service dogs.

Freedom Fidos takes pride in this accomplishment and is hopeful for other states to do the same. Contact Freedom Fidos how to start a proclamation request in your state.

Below is a copy of Governor Kemp's signed proclamation.

BY THE GOVERNOR OF THE STATE OF GEORGIA

A PROCLAMATION

SERVICE DOGS FOR VETERANS
AWARENESS WEEK

WHEREAS: The State of Georgia is committed to providing all possible assistance to its many accomplished, respected, and well-known veterans who become disabled through their service to our nation; and

WHEREAS: Disabled veterans endure a wide variety of conditions as a direct result of their military service, including vision and/or hearing loss, physical injuries, traumatic brain injuries, post-traumatic stress disorder, and seizures; and

WHEREAS: Well-trained service dogs allow veterans to lead more independent lives through their assistance with mobility, medical alert, carrying and retrieving needed objects, and guidework; and

WHEREAS: The public benefits from organizations like Freedom Fidos that train service dogs, provide knowledge of the important roles service dogs play, and teach proper etiquette to individuals who own service dogs and those who encounter them; and

WHEREAS: By promoting education, employment, housing, and recreation opportunities for disabled veterans with service dogs, we can maximize their chances for a productive life; and

WHEREAS: It is appropriate to celebrate the achievements of veterans who are disabled and further raise awareness of their needs; now

THEREFORE: I, BRIAN P. KEMP, Governor of the State of Georgia, do hereby proclaim October 6-12, 2019 as SERVICE DOGS FOR VETERANS AWARENESS WEEK in Georgia.

In witness thereof, I have hereunto set my hand and caused the Seal of the Executive Department to be affixed this 18th day of July in the year of our Lord, Two Thousand and Nineteen.

_____
GOVERNOR

ATTEST

_____
CHIEF OF STAFF

APPENDIX A

APPENDIX A

POLICIES, REGULATIONS
AND LAWS
Lit. Compiled
(Unedited)

AMERICANS WITH DISABILITIES ACT
(Service Animals)

The Department of Justice published revised final regulations implementing the Americans with Disabilities Act (ADA) for title II (State and local government services) and title III (public accommodations and commercial facilities) on September 15, 2010, in the Federal Register. These requirements, or rules, clarify and refine issues that have arisen over the past 20 years and contain new, and updated, requirements, including the 2010 Standards for Accessible Design (2010 Standards).

Overview:
This publication provides guidance on the term "service animal" and the service animal provisions in the Department's new regulations.

- Beginning on March 15, 2011, **only dogs are recognized** as service animals under titles II and III of the ADA.
- **A service animal** is a dog that is individually trained to do work or perform tasks for a person with a disability.
- Generally, title II and title III entities must permit service animals to accompany people with disabilities in all areas where members of the public are allowed to go.

How "Service Animal" Is Defined:

Service animals are defined as dogs that are individually trained to do work or perform tasks for people with disabilities. Examples of such work or tasks include guiding people who are blind, alerting people who are deaf, pulling a wheelchair, alerting and protecting a person who is having a seizure, reminding a person with mental illness to take prescribed medications, calming a person with *Post Traumatic Stress Disorder* (PTSD) during an anxiety attack, or performing other duties. Service animals are working animals, not pets. The work or task a dog has been trained to provide must be directly related to the person's disability.

Dogs whose sole function is to provide comfort or emotional support do not qualify as service animals under the ADA.

This definition does not affect or limit the broader definition of "assistance animal" under the Fair Housing Act or the broader definition of "service animal" under the Air Carrier Access Act.

Some State and local laws also define service animal more broadly than the ADA does.

Information about such laws can be obtained from the State attorney general's office.

Where Service Animals Are Allowed:

Under the ADA, State and local governments, businesses, and nonprofit organizations that serve the public generally must allow service animals to accompany people with disabilities in all areas of the facility where the public is normally allowed to go. For example, in a hospital, it would be inappropriate to exclude a service animal from areas such as patient rooms, clinics, cafeterias, or examination rooms. However, it may be appropriate to exclude a service animal from operating rooms or burn units where the animal's presence may compromise a sterile environment.

Service Animals Must Be Under Control:
Under the ADA, service animals must be harnessed, leashed, or tethered, unless these devices interfere with the service animal's work or the individual's disability prevents using these devices. In that case, the individual must maintain control of the animal through voice, signal, or other effective controls.

Inquiries, Exclusions, Charges, and Other Specific Rules Related to Service Animals:
- When it is not obvious what service an animal provides, only limited inquiries are allowed. Staff may ask two questions: (1) is the dog a service animal required because of a disability, and (2) what work, or task has the dog been trained to perform. Staff cannot ask about the person's disability, require medical documentation, require a special identification card or training documentation for the dog, or ask that the dog demonstrate its ability to perform the work or task.
- Allergies and fear of dogs are not valid reasons for denying access or refusing service to people using service animals. When a person who is allergic to dog dander and a person who uses a service animal must spend time in the same room or facility, for example, in a school classroom or at a homeless shelter, they both should be accommodated by assigning them, if possible, to different locations within the room or different rooms in the facility.
- A person with a disability cannot be asked to remove his service animal from the premises unless: (1) the dog is out of control and the handler does not take effective action to control it or (2) the dog is not housebroken. When there is a legitimate reason to ask that a service animal be removed, staff must offer the person with the disability the opportunity to obtain goods or services without the animal's presence.

- Establishments that sell or prepare food must allow service animals in public areas even if state or local health codes prohibit animals on the premises.
- People with disabilities who use service animals cannot be isolated from other patrons, treated less favorably than other patrons, or charged fees that are not charged to other patrons without animals. In addition, if a business requires a deposit or fee to be paid by patrons with pets, it must waive the charge for service animals.
- If a business such as a hotel normally charges guests for damage that they cause, a customer with a disability may also be charged for damage caused by himself or his service animal.
- Staff is not required to provide care or food for a service animal.

Miniature Horses:

In addition to the provisions about service dogs, the Department's revised ADA regulations have a new, separate provision about miniature horses that have been individually trained to do work or perform tasks for people with disabilities. (Miniature horses generally range in height from 24 inches to 34 inches measured to the shoulders and generally weigh between 70 and 100 pounds.) Entities covered by the ADA must modify their policies to permit miniature horses where reasonable. The regulations set out four assessment factors to assist entities in determining whether miniature horses can be accommodated in their facility. The assessment factors are (1) whether the miniature horse is housebroken; (2) whether the miniature horse is under the owner's control; (3) whether the facility can accommodate the miniature horse's type, size, and weight; and (4) whether the miniature horse's presence will not compromise legitimate safety requirements necessary for safe operation of the facility.

For more information about the ADA, please visit our website or call our toll-free number (see below):

ADA Website: www.ADA.gov

To receive e-mail notifications when new ADA information is available: visit the ADA Website's home page and click the link near the top of the middle column.

ADA Information Line: 1-800-514-0301 (Voice) and 1-800-514-0383 (TTY)
M-W, F 9:30 a.m. – 5:30 p.m., Th 12:30 p.m. – 5:30 p.m. (Eastern Time)
All calls are confidential.

For persons with disabilities, this publication is available in alternate formats.

The Americans with Disabilities Act authorizes the Department of Justice (the Department) to provide technical assistance to individuals and entities that have rights or responsibilities under the Act. This document provides informal guidance to assist you in understanding the ADA and the Department's regulations.

This guidance document is not intended to be a final agency action, has no legally binding effect, and may be rescinded or modified in the Department's complete discretion, in accordance with applicable laws. The Department's guidance documents, including this guidance, do not establish legally enforceable responsibilities beyond what is required by the terms of the applicable statutes, regulations, or binding judicial precedent.

DISABILITY LAW CENTER
(Including Service Dogs' Rights in Housing, Employment, Access in Utah)

The Origins of Protection & Advocacy (P&A) and Cap Systems
P&As were established to address public outcry in response to the abuse, neglect, and lack of programming in institutions for persons with disabilities. Congress has created distinct statutory programs to address the needs of different populations of persons with disabilities. The governor in each state designated an agency to be the P&A system and provided assurance that the system was and would remain independent of any service provider. **There is a federally mandated system** *in each state and territory* that provides protection to ensure the civil and human of the rights of persons with disabilities through legally based advocacy.

The Disability Law Center (DLC) is a private non-profit organization designated by the governor to protect the rights of people with disabilities in Utah. The Disability Law Center opened in 1978, shortly after the P&A system was established. There are several core federally mandated programs and funding sources, which the DLC uses to operate: The Protection and Advocacy for the Developmental Disabilities program (PADD), the Protection and Advocacy for Individuals with Mental Illness (PAIMI), Protection and Advocacy for Individual Rights (PAIR), the Client Assistance Program (CAP), Protection and Advocacy for Beneficiaries of Social Security (PABSS) , Protection and Advocacy for Traumatic Brain Injury (PATBI), Protection and Advocacy for Assistive Technology and Protection and Advocacy for Voting Access (PAVA). The DLC also receives funding from a variety of private foundations and individuals.

The Disability Law Center's Mission, Vision, and Long-Range Goals
The Disability Law Center is the only agency that provides self-advocacy assistance, disability rights education, on-site monitoring and investigation of programs and facilities, and systemic advocacy, and legal services on behalf of the more than 300,000 people with disabilities in Utah.

The mission of the Disability Law Center is to enforce and strengthen laws that protect the opportunities, choices and legal rights of people with disabilities in Utah.

The DLC's advocacy is geared toward improving the lives of Utahns with disabilities by ending abuse and neglect, ending discrimination, creating opportunities for employment, and increasing access to services. We create the change we envision by empowering people through information, hands-on training, legal action, and ongoing support. Our work strives to create a society where abilities, rather than disabilities, are recognized; all people have an equal opportunity to participate; and where all are treated with equity, dignity, and respect.

Legal Advocacy
The Disability Law Center provides legal advocacy services. These include:
1. Information and referral
2. Short Term Assistance
3. Information on disability law and related rights
4. Investigation and monitoring of abuse and neglect in residential facilities
5. Mediation and negotiation
6. Presentations and outreach
7. Representation in administrative hearings and court proceedings
8. Class action litigation
9. Self-advocacy support and training

In addition, P&A systems interact with elected and appointed officials to share information which will assist policymakers in making legislative and administrative changes which benefit persons with disabilities.

Legally based advocacy for persons with disabilities are based on the following principles:

Equality, Equity, and Fairness
People with disabilities are full and equal citizens under the law. They are entitled to equal access to the same opportunities afforded all members of society. People with disabilities are entitled to be free from abuse, neglect, exploitation, discrimination, and isolation, and to be treated with respect and dignity.

Meaningful Choice and Empowerment
People, regardless of age, type and level of disability have the right to make choices both with respect to daily routines and major life events.

Supports and Participation
Services and supports are shaped by the unique needs and preferences of each individual and assure and enhance opportunities for integration in all aspects of life. Services are age-appropriate and premised on the fact that people with disabilities, continue to learn, change and develop throughout their lives. For children such growth is best accomplished within families, and for adults, within integrated communities, rather than institutions.

Independence
Advocacy services are based on a philosophy of equal access, peer support and self-determination to be achieved through individual, professional and system advocacy. Services are delivered in a manner that maximizes leadership, independence, productivity, and integration of individuals with disabilities.

Cultural Competency
Advocacy services reflect and are responsive to, the diverse cultural, ethnic and racial composition of Utah.

Getting Help
DLC services are free of charge and available to anyone who has a disability living in the state of Utah. Although the areas of focus may change from year to year, the DLC remains dedicated to enforcing and strengthening laws that protect the opportunities, choices, and legal rights of people with disabilities in Utah. The DLC always welcome suggestions for new areas of focus.
To view our current priorities, please visit our website at http://disabiltylawcenter.org/priorities

In other states, call 211 to ask for your disability law center in your area.

Contact us at:
Disability Law Center
205 North 400 West
Salt Lake City, UT 84103
(800) 662-9080 phone
(801) 363-1437 fax

Intake Hours
MON-THURS: 9:00am-4:00pm (calls/walk-ins)
FRIDAY: 9:00am-1:00pm (calls/walk-ins); 1:00pm-4:00pm (walk-ins only)

Video Relay Services
Contact us for free by video relay, visit Sorenson Video Relay Services.

SERVICE ANIMAL THROUGH AIRPORT SECURITY
(TSA)

Traveling by air with your service animal is a straightforward process. You and your service animal can travel together as long as your service animal is small enough to sit by your feet or under the seat in front of you without obstructing aisles and exit pathways provided it is a type of animal permitted on US air carriers. Preparing for the airport security screening process will help you and your service animal go through without difficulty.

Familiarize yourself with the applicable regulations and procedures before you go to the airport.

Quarantine Regulations:
If you are traveling to an island destination, such as Hawaii, Jamaica, the United Kingdom or Australia, you should carefully review animal quarantine rules and procedures for guide and service animals. This is true even if you are only passing through the airport. You may need to begin the compliance process several months before your departure date, particularly if you are visiting the UK.

TSA Procedures:
The Transportation Security Administration (TSA) must comply with all federal regulations pertaining to service animals. The TSA has established procedures for screening service animals, with specific guidelines for service dogs and service monkeys. You must tell the screening officer that you are traveling with a service animal, and both you and your service animal must go through a metal detector and/or be patted down. If you know what to expect during the airport security screening process, you and your service animal will be able to quickly go through the security checkpoint.

Airline Service Animal Policies:
Your airline may have established specific policies for passengers traveling with service animals. For example, American Airlines asks passengers to check in one hour early if they are accompanied by a service animal. They also require 48 hours' notice from passengers planning to bring service animals onto the aircraft. This helps airline personnel seat passengers with service animals in appropriate areas, such as bulkhead seats, and position them far from passengers with animal allergies. Call your airline or consult its website as far in advance as possible to find out how to notify your airline of your upcoming trip.

Travel and Federal Law:
Passengers traveling on US carriers with service animals are protected under the Air Carrier Access Act (ACAA), also known as Title 14 CFR Part 382. Under these laws, airline personnel cannot require you to transport your service animal in the cargo hold unless it is too large to sit at your feet in the bulkhead section or under the seat in front of you during the flight. Airline employees may ask you about your service animal and may require you to show documentation provided by a licensed medical professional if you are traveling with an emotional support animal or psychiatric service animal.

Large service animals may need to travel in the cargo hold unless you are able and willing to buy a second ticket to accommodate your animal companion. In addition, US law does not require airlines to transport snakes, ferrets, rodents, or spiders, even if they are considered service animals, because they can carry diseases.

Emotional support animals are considered to be in a different category than service animals under the Air Carrier Access Act. You must provide written documentation of your need for an emotional support animal from your licensed mental health professional, and your airline may require you to give at least 48 hours' notice that you will be traveling with your emotional support animal.

Prepare for Airport Security:
As you pack your bags and get ready to head toward the airport, take a few extra minutes to make sure you are ready to go through airport security with your service animal. If you travel frequently, consider signing up for TSA PreCheck.

Also, remember to tell your airline about your service animal no later than 48 hours before your flight.

Remember that you, too, must go through airport security. Wear slip-on shoes, if possible, and be ready to take your laptop out of its case. Empty your pockets. Put your change, keys, and other metal objects into your carry-on bag to avoid setting off the metal detector.

Keep your printed or electronic ticket, identification, passport and service animal documentation in an easy-to-reach spot. You will need to produce these items at least twice during a typical security screening.

Take a Potty Break:
Take your service animal to the airport's pet relief area outside before you check in for your flight and go through security. There are available pet relief areas at some airports (usually, there are two indoor pet relief areas). Go to www.petfriendlytravel.com website to find your airports' pet relief areas.

Be Flexible:
As you go through the screening area, you may be asked to walk through the metal detector with your service animal rather than separately. This means that both of you will need extra screening if the alarm sounds. If you travel with a service monkey, you may be asked to remove its diaper. Remember that TSA security screeners

are trained to let you handle your service animal; they should not touch it or talk to it. They will, however, screen any saddlebags your service animal wears and use a wand and or pat down its leash and other accessories.

Security screeners will expect you to control your service animal during this process.

Resolve Problems Appropriately:
Every airline has a Complaint Resolution Officer (CRO) who should be available in person or by telephone to help resolve problems. You can ask to speak to the CRO if you are having difficulty with your airline's boarding process. In addition, the US Department of Transportation has an aviation consumers' disability hotline you can call if you are experiencing difficulty. The telephone number is (800) 778-4348 and the TTY number is (800) 455-9880.

On the Airplane:
As you board, guide your service animal to your seat or ask a flight attendant to direct you. You may be asked to move if your assigned seat is in an exit row or if you are seated near a passenger with animal allergies. The flight attendants should make every effort to accommodate both you and any allergic passengers. Remember to ask to speak to the CRO if significant problems arise.

The Bottom Line:
Know your rights under the law and bring a smile with you to the airport. Preparation, organization, good manners, and flexibility will help you get through airport security and onto your airplane without problems. To learn more about TSA go to www.Tsa.gov website.

The Association of Flight Attendants, citing a survey of about 5,000 flight attendants across 30 airlines, 61% worked flights where emotional support animal caused a disturbance, and one in four flight attendants had to deal with animals defecating or urinating in the cabin, while 13% reported animal-related conflict among the passengers.

The union is hoping the survey results will push the federal government to adopt tighter regulations on what animals may fly on commercial airlines, its officials said.

Sara Nelson, the union's president, said the survey suggests the problem is getting further out of hand while the Transportation Department considers new rules. More than 98% of the survey's respondents worked on a flight with at least one emotional support animal in the past two years, and many of those were not fun.

The responses we got from the survey only heighten our concern because of the number of flight attendants who were saying that the animals got loose that they were acting aggressively toward other passengers, and frankly, the number that were defecating and urinating in the cabin. That's a serious health issue," Nelson said in an interview Thursday.

The issue is such a hot topic for flight attendants at the moment that the union's survey reached beyond its own to include flight crews at airlines it doesn't represent, she said.

The AFA argues that so many animals on flights is not only making life unpleasant for crews and passengers, it's fueling a growing backlash against all in-flight animals, including bona fide service animals that are trained to help people with disabilities.

One flight attendant was bitten on the foot as she walked past a dog, and another was bitten while placing a drink on a tray table. Nelson was on a flight where a dog walked back and forth across several passengers, to everyone's amusement – until the dog became worked up and began acting aggressively. The mood of nearby passengers also changed for the worse, she said.

"And at one point the owner had to contain the animal because what started as a very happy, cuddly situation for whatever reason turned into a stressful situation for the animal," Nelson said. "That owner was able to get that animal under control, but that's not always the case."

It's not just dogs, either. Delta Airlines, which announced this year that it was implementing stricter rules, said people have tried to fly with companion turkeys, companion snakes, companion spiders and more. The AFA said a bird got loose on one flight and couldn't be found in the cabin for 45 minutes.

The union also is raising concern about the welfare of animals brought aboard planes improperly. Unlike trained service animals, pets and other creatures are generally not acclimated to the stressful conditions of commercial flight, including cramped spaces and cabin pressurization, Nelson said. Some animals become anxious and aggressive under such conditions.

"If it's really a service animal, they are trained to be in that space. They are trained for emergency situations," Nelson said.

The union, which represents more than 50,000 flight attendants at 20 airlines, said its membership backs new regulations that might permit some emotional support animals aboard a flight, but only if they are strictly licensed and certified and required to be kept under proper control — all characteristics of properly trained service animals, which the union welcomes.

"I will you tell that, actually, some of our favorite animals are service animals," Nelson said. "You wouldn't even know that they're there. They're trained to almost make themselves invisible and to give their owners the care and the guidance that they need.

But these emotional support animals are not trained to be in these spaces."

Delta's move, announced Friday, suggests we may yet return to sanity. The airline said that as of March 1, it will start requiring advance documentation before boarding animals to certify the owner's need and the animal's training. The airline said it adopted the new policy to ensure the safety of its staff, other passengers, and trained service animals.

"Customers have attempted to fly with comfort turkeys, gliding possums known as sugar gliders, snakes, spiders and more," Delta said in its announcement. The airline said it took steps after an 84-percent increase in unpleasant, unsanitary or dangerous incidents with animals on planes since 2016, including a 70-pound dog's attack on a passenger.

Best of all, Marx went undercover for her story, taking various emotional support animals on jaunts around town, including a trip to some art galleries with an alpaca. She took a pig on an airplane. No one forcibly dragged the pig off the flight, by the way, even when it was acting like one.

It was all a great con, and one that thousands of other people pull off everyday with differing amounts of insincere sincerity. Over at Animalia, my colleague Karin Brulliard says the Department of Transportation's regular reports on disability-related complaints show that those involving service animals nearly quadrupled between 2012 and 2016. She also notes that 19 states have passed laws that criminalize passing off pets as service animals.

What's going on here is selfishness dressed up to look like a love for animals. Besides, what does it say about the American psyche that in a nation that has endured the Great Depression, two world wars, a Cold War and many other crises, so many people can't board an airplane without their pet at their side? Isn't that why they make stuffed animals?

The writer, Patricia Marx, drew a proper distinction between bona fide service animals — which are trained to perform certain tasks for their owners, such as guide dogs for the blind, or dogs that respond to their owners' seizures — and loosely certified emotional support animals, which she said were essentially "blankies."

DELTA IS TIGHTENING RESTRICTIONS ON SERVICE ANIMALS
Lit.-1/22/2018 by Fredrick Kunkle

IT'S ABOUT TIME!
Delta deserves praise for its recent decision to impose tighter restrictions on service animals. Here's hoping the other airlines will follow suit.

The epidemic that has led to animals showing up in places where they don't belong has been going on for a while now. It's been abetted by loopholes in well-meaning legislation, such as the Americans with Disabilities Act and the Air Carrier Access Act, that were intended to make sure that people who have disabilities and their trained service animals would be able to get around without hassles. But many pet owners, not to mention a bunch of online registration companies, have taken advantage of the law.

The New Yorker took a droll look at the abuses a few years ago. Among the many anecdotes of animals excess the magazine reported was one about how Ivana Trump let her miniature Yorkie romp at a fancy Italian restaurant in New York. Ivana, too, claimed the pup was a service animal, the New Yorker says.

Congress will consider tightening the rules on service animals allowed to accompany passengers on airliners under legislation introduced this week.

Sen. Richard Burr (R-N.C.) has introduced an airline bill that would align the definition of a service animal to fit the stricter regulations in the Americans With Disabilities Act (ADA).

Burr, noting that things have gotten out of hand when people try bringing support kangaroos onto a plane, said in a news release that the proposed rule would also establish a criminal penalty for falsely asserting that the family pet is a service animal.

ALLERGIES SUGGESTION
Airlines decided to revise their own rules after a Transportation Department panel was unable to reach a regulatory compromise in 2016.

"Recently, a few airlines have begun requiring service animal users to provide information about their animal's health and behavior as a condition of travel," the department said. It's also recommended that all passengers who are allergic to animals to request not to be seated next to animals when checking in at the airport gates. This will refrain from departure delays.

In January, Delta said its changes came as the airline carried about 250,000 animals last year that were increasingly misbehaving by wandering the cabin, defecating or even biting passengers. A comfort dog bit a passenger in the face while a flight boarded last June.

United's change in February came after a woman tried to bring a peacock with her on a flight. But United began reviewing its policy in 2017 after noticing a jump in comfort animals on flights to

76,000 from 43,000 the year before and "a significant increase in onboard incidents."

Starting July 1, American will require passengers to notify the carrier about a comfort animal 48 hours before a flight and then sign a waiver stating the need for the animal.

In order for an animal to qualify, the passenger must provide a letter from a mental-health professional describing the mental or emotional disability that shows the need for the animal and proof of the professional's licensing. Then, there's the Air Carrier Access Act, which governs air travel. It's similar to the FHA in that it mandates access for ESAs and allows airlines to ask for proof. And, that creates two major problems:

- It has created a cottage industry for scammers and profiteers selling ESA certificates to anybody who wants one.
- People tend to conflate it with the ADA and assume they are allowed to bring their ESA into all public places. Froufrou is peeing on the chips at your local supermarket right now because her owner mistakenly believes that they're entitled to bring her along simply because their unethical mental health professional wrote a letter saying she can fly in their lap or because they purchased such a certificate online. And, due to an overwhelming sense of entitlement and selfishness, too. Obviously.

WHAT THE DEPARTMENT OF TRANSPORTATION (DOT) IS DOING ABOUT IT
Delta, United, and American have all announced major changes to their emotional support animal policies this year. They've banned exotic animals, like emotional support tarantulas or peacocks, and have created online documentation centers that formalize the approval process for onboard animals in an attempt to prevent people from flagrantly gaming the system with nothing but a

verbal promise that Froufrou is an ESA. The DOT has said it's okay with the airlines doing this, even if it's technically in violation of the ACAA.

That has necessarily led to a review of the ACAA itself. "The Department has heard from the transportation industry, as well as individuals with disabilities, that the current ACAA regulation could be improved to ensure nondiscriminatory access for individuals with disabilities, while simultaneously preventing instances of fraud and ensuring consistency with other Federal regulations," states the DOT, announcing its review of the law.

A public comment period that opened on May 17 has received 1,521 comments to date. It's open through July 9.

Identifying the need for new rulemaking, the DOT references fraud, the presence of untrained animals on flights, and the urinating, defecating, and biting that their presence inevitably leads to. Requests for this review came from both the Psychiatric Service Dog Association, which is worried about discrimination against the disabled, and Airlines for America, an airline industry lobbying group.

Justifying its request for the ACAA review, Airlines for America states, "The DOT providing a better understanding on issues like the definition of service animals, or what they mean when they direct prompt service for disabled passengers, allows our industry the opportunity to improve. We're not trying to charge for these things or mitigate costs. We want to have a better understanding, so we can provide better service to communities that deserve every consideration."

Solutions being suggested by industry stakeholders and lobby groups run from an outright ban on ESAs in airline cabins to a greater burden of proof on people claiming a legitimate need for their dogs. Mandating that ESAs remain confined to pet carriers, limiting the number of ESAs per passenger, and creating a formalized burden of training are also being discussed.

"Things need to change," states Airlines for America. Whatever that change may be, one thing seems clear: It's going to get harder to fly with a fake service dog. Thank God.

UPDATES
DOT 48-19

Thursday, August 08, 2019

U.S. Department of Transportation Issues Final Statement of Enforcement Priorities Regarding Service Animals on Flights

WASHINGTON – The U.S. Department of Transportation (DOT) today issued a Final Statement of Enforcement Priorities Regarding Service Animals (link) that provides greater clarity to passengers, airlines, and other stakeholders about the DOT's interpretation and enforcement of the existing service animal rules.

In this Final Statement, the Department's Enforcement Office announced that it does not intend to take action against an airline for asking users of any type of service animal to provide documentation related to vaccination, training, or behavior so long as it is reasonable to believe that the documentation would assist the airline in making a determination as to whether an animal poses a direct threat to the health or safety of others. The Enforcement Office will monitor airlines' animal documentation requirements to ensure that they are reasonable.

The Final Statement also addresses a number of other issues, such as species limitations, containment, advance notice, and check-in requirements for Emotional Support and Psychiatric Service Animals: The statement can be found at: https://www.transportation.gov/airconsumer/latest-news

https://www.transportation.gov/airconsumer/disability

The Department remains committed to ensuring that our air transportation system is safe and accessible for everyone. As such, the Enforcement Office will focus its enforcement efforts on clear violations of the current rule and will continue to investigate all complaints alleging violations of the Air Carrier Access Act.

Separately, DOT plans to issue a Notice of Proposed Rulemaking on Service Animals later this year.

The final statement can be found at regulations.gov, docket number DOT-OST-2018-0067. 0 It is effective upon publication in the Federal Register. Airlines are expected to review their policies and revise them, if necessary, to comply with the Department's disability regulation.

Final Statement of Enforcement Priorities Regarding Service Animals - Summary

- Species Limitations: The Department's disability regulation has a broad definition of service animals. Priority will be placed on ensuring that the most commonly recognized service animals (dogs, cats and miniature horses) are accepted for transport. Nevertheless, airlines are still subject to enforcement action if they categorically refuse to transport other species that they are required to transport under the current rule.
- Breed/Species Restrictions: The Department's Enforcement Office views a limitation based exclusively on breed of the service animal to not be allowed under its service animal regulation. The Enforcement Office intends to use available resources to ensure that dogs as a species are accepted for

transport. Airlines are permitted to find that any specific animal, regardless of breed, poses a direct threat.

- Documentation Requirements: The Department's disability regulation permits airlines to determine, in advance of flight, whether any service animal poses a direct threat, but the rule does not clearly indicate how airlines must make that assessment. The Department's Enforcement Office does not intend to take action against an airline for asking users of any type of service animal to present documentation related to the service animal's vaccination, training or behavior so long as it is reasonable to believe that the documentation would assist the airline in making a determination as to whether an animal poses a direct threat to the health or safety of others. The Enforcement Office will monitor the airlines' animal documentation requirements to ensure that they are not being used to unduly restrict passengers with disabilities from traveling with their service animals.

- Containment: The Department's disability regulation contains no explicit requirements or prohibitions with respect to containment of service animals in the cabin. The Department's Enforcement Office will consider containment issues for all service animals on a case-by-case basis, with a focus on reasonableness. In general, tethering and similar means of controlling an animal that are permitted in the Americans with Disabilities Act context would be reasonable in the context of controlling service animals in the aircraft cabin.

- Advance Notice: The Department's disability regulation prohibits airlines from requiring advance notice for passengers traveling with service animals, other than emotional support animals (ESAs) and psychiatric support animals (PSAs). Enforcement resources will be focused on ensuring that airlines do not require advance notice for passengers with traditional service animals as advance notice may significantly harm passengers with disabilities as it prevents them from making last minute travel plans that may be necessary for work or family emergencies.

- Check-In Requirements: The Department's Enforcement Office does not view it to be violation of the Department's disability regulation if airlines require lobby check-in for ESAs and PSAs because the regulation permits airlines to require ESA and PSA users to check in one hour before the check-in time for the general public.

- Proof that an Animal is a Service Animal: The Department's Enforcement Office has long interpreted existing law as permitting airlines to seek credible verbal assurance that a passenger is an individual with a disability and the animal is a service animal. If a passenger's disability is not clear, airlines may ask questions to determine the passenger's need for the animal even if the animal has other indicia of a service animal such as a harness, vest or tag.

- Number of Service Animals Per Passenger: The Department's disability regulation is not clear as to how many service animals may travel with a passenger with a disability. Enforcement efforts will generally focus on ensuring that airlines are not restricting passengers from traveling with one ESA and a total of three service animals if needed. Generally, one ESA should be sufficient for emotional support, but a passenger may reasonably need more than one task-trained service animal.

- Number of Service Animals per Aircraft: The Department's disability regulation does not allow airlines to deny transport to a service animal accompanying a passenger with a disability because of a limit on the total number of service animals that can be on any flight. The Department's Enforcement Office would thus view denial of transport to an ESA because of other ESAs in the cabin of aircraft to violate its regulation as ESAs are considered service animals under the existing rule.

- Weight Restrictions: Under the Department's disability regulation, airlines may deny transport to a service animal that is too large or too heavy to be accommodated in the cabin The Department's Enforcement Office views a categorical ban on animals over a certain weight limit, regardless of the type of aircraft for the flight, to be inconsistent with the regulation.

- Age Restrictions: The Department's disability regulation does not address the minimum age of a service animal. However, all service animals (including ESAs) are expected to be trained to behave in public. As a general matter, the Department's Enforcement Office would not view it to be a violation for an airline to prohibit the transport of service animals younger than four months as some airlines have done.

- Flight-Length Restrictions: The Department's disability regulation provides that airlines may require passengers using a service animal on flights scheduled to take eight hours or more to provide documentation that the animal will not need to relieve itself on the flight or that it can do so in a way that does not create a health or sanitation issue on the flight. The Department's Enforcement Office intends to use its available resources to ensure that airlines comply with the existing regulations with respect to this issue and do not automatically prohibit service animals (including ESAs) on flights lasting eight or more hours.

- Mental Health Professional Form: Under the Department's disability regulation, airlines are not required to transport ESAs or PSAs unless the passenger provides medical documentation of their need for the animal as specified in the rule. The Department's Enforcement Office would view it to be a violation for an airline to reject a medical form or letter that meets the criteria found in the rule because of an airline's preference that the passenger use the airline's form.

APPENDIX B

APPENDIX B

(Limited Available Space Limits Resources)

RESOURCES AND TIPS
Aziza Rodriguez, Janet Ingber, and R.Rice

Financial Aid Resources

Best Friends

www.bestfriends.org/resources/financial-aid-pets

This site offers a list of programs by state that may offer financial assistance based on service dog status, low income, or emergency and critical need.

AAHA Helping Pets Fund

http://aahahelpingpetsfund.org

Angels4Animals

https://angels4animals.org/index.html

Care Credit (No interest plan for veterinary care)

https://www.carecredit.com/

Animal/Pet Care: Unlike traditional pet financing or veterinary payment plans, the CareCredit credit card gives you the flexibility to use your card again and again for your pet's procedures. For more information call 1-866-893-7864

Chewy

www.chewy.com
Offers prescriptions by mail at reasonable rates

Guide Dog Users of Canada

https://gduc.ca

Maintains a Wellness Fund in order to assist those individuals in financial need, partnered with guide dogs, with veterinary expenses that are not routine. Applicants must meet specified requirements at the time of application.

Help A Pet
http://www.help-a-pet.org/

IMOM
https://www.imom.org/

Labrador Life Line
http://www.labradorlifeline.org/

Pet Assure
1-888-789-7387
www.petassure.com

Pet Assure offers an alternative to purchasing insurance plans via a card that helps you take advantage of discounted in-house medical services and procedures provided by veterinary clinics signed up with their program. It is possible to refer clinics to the program if they are not already registered. This program is run off of a monthly fee, no deductibles and can be used an unlimited amount of times as long as your account is active. An added benefit is that specific pet related merchant discounts are available to Pet Assured members.

PetMeds
1-800-PetMeds (738-6337)
www.1800petmeds.com

While not specifically offering any service dog related discounts, this company can sometimes offer more affordable prices on medications and supplements. The company also has a mobile app available on both the app store and google play store, developed by PetMed Express.

Pet Plan
1-800-242-7129
www.gopetplan.com

A pet insurance provider which offers service dog owners a 5% discount on the overall quote, which is determined by dog breed, age and location.

Shakespeare Pet Fund
https://www.shakespearepetfun.org/

The Pet Fund
https://www.thepetfund.com/

Trupanion
1-888-733-2685
www.trupanion.com/pet-insurance/working-pets

A pet insurance provider that recognizes the level of care service animals are given directly correlates to the cost of emergency care. Trupanion's working dog premiums are less costly than coverage of play pets

United Animal Nations – Lifeline Program
https://www.uan.org/index.cfm?navid=163#National-organizations
Veterans: Service Dog Veterinary Health Benefit:
www.prosthetics.va.gov

Will recognize service dogs for insurance benefit: Hearing, Guide, Mobility, and Mental Health.

<u>Other websites available to search for veterinary care assistance</u>:

https://humanesociety.org/animals/resources/tips/trouble_affording_veterinary_care.html

https://needhelpayingbills.com/html/help_with_vet_and_pet_bills.html

Food and Supplies

Chewy
1-800-672-4399
www.chewy.com

Chewy offers a wide range of pet supplies and has excellent customer service. Shipping, when fees are applied, is more than manageable, and only a handful of states are charged a sales tax. Returns are handled with efficiency and with minimal hassle.

Pet Flow
Main line: 1-888-316-7297
Accessibility Line: 1-844-834-7297
www.PetFlow.com

Pet Flow is another online retailer that offers a wide range of pet supplies, including food and prescription medications. While no discounts are provided for service dogs, users can earn $10 off their order for every person they invite to join the platform. Furthermore, Pet Flow donates a bowl of food to a pet in need for every order shipped to their customers.
Referral Link: http://ref.petflow.com/mA-LM

Ruffwear
1-888-783-3932
https://ruffwear.com/

Ruffwear provides customers with reliable gear for winter and summer travel for active dogs. Service dog handlers and affiliate dog trainers can qualify for 40% off site prices by applying for their Pro Purchase Program.
Application can be found: https://ruffwear.com/pages/pro-purchase-program

Muttluks
1-888-MUTTLUK (688-8585)

muttluks@muttluks.com
https://muttluks.com/

Muttluks' Woof Wish Program provides 50% discounts to service dog handlers for shoes and coats. Customers must email or call for an applicable code.

K9 Top Coat
https://k9topcoat.com/

This company provides well-made coats for dogs working in extreme temperatures or who are susceptible to the cold due to thinner fur. The costs range in design from general protection from rain to full body coverage from snow and ice. K9 Top Coat does not offer any specific service dog related discounts at this time.

Darwin's Pet Food
1-877-738-6325
info@darwinspet.com
https://www.darwinspet.com/

Darwin's Pet Food offers service dog handlers and accredited animal professionals discounts on all-natural raw dog food. Customers access the program by emailing customer service.

On the Go
http://www.guide-and-service-dogs.com

Julie Johnson provides well-made gear for service dog handlers. Pieces can be made to order, and fit different life styles. On the Go can also be found on the Blindmicemall.com platform.

Mutt Muffs
1-443-536-6287
http://www.safeandsoundpets.com/index.html

Mutt Muffs provide ear protection for dogs working in extremely noisy environments. These muffs can also help dogs affected by airplane travel, fireworks, and sometimes thunder storms—they do not affect the dog's ability to hear handler commands.

What Dog Food to Choose?
www.DogFoodAdivsor.com

The Dog Food Advisor's unbiased dog food reviews and ratings searchable by brand and star rating. Candid reviews, trusted advice and lifesaving recall alerts.

Emergency and First Aid Resources

Pet First Aid by American Red Cross

This app allows users to read up on first aid and emergency techniques as well as take quizzes on what they have learned. Videos and step by step instruction are also available for people with different learning styles. This app is on the Amazon App Store and Google Play.

Pet Poison Helpline
1- 855-764-7661
Puerto Rico or the US Virgin Islands: 877-416-7319.
Other Caribbean islands: 011-1-952-853-1716
www.petpoisonhelpline.com

A 24-hour service available in the U.S., Canada, and the Caribbean's designed to assist with animal poison control. The $59 fee per case is waved for service dogs.

Knowing Your Rights

Air Carrier Access Act (ACAA)
1-855-368-4200
https://www.transportation.gov/tags/air-carrier-access-act

(Update ESA requirements)

Americans with Disabilities Act (ADA)
1-800-514-0301 (Voice)
1-800-514-0383 (TTY)
www.ada.gov
(Housing, employment, access)

Department of Homeland Security (DHS)
Office for Civil Rights and Civil Liberties
Mail Stop #0800
245 Murray Lane, S.W., Bldg. 41
Washington, D.C. 20598
(For complaints regarding security checkpoints)

Disability Law Center (DLC UTAH)
Each state has their own federally-funded Disability Law Center.
(Call your state's 211 for assistance)

Guide Dog Users, Inc. (GDUI)
1-866-799-8436
president@gdui.org

(Largest advocacy organization for guide dog users in the United States and strives to promote civil rights and enhance the quality of life for working guide dog teams.)

Guide Dog Users of Canada (GDUC)
https://gduc.ca

Guide Dog Users of Canada provides a forum for those wishing to give or receive Peer Support; educate the public about the abilities of Guide Dogs, and the rights of those partnered with guide dogs; promotes the high standards and integrity of guide dog training; and assists with individual or systemic advocacy whenever necessary.

International Association of Assistance Dog Partners (IAADP) - Access Issues
www.iaadp.org/access.html

This resource lists the responsibilities of handlers outlined in service dog related laws when traveling, taking into account mandatory Quarantines, and medical requirements. IAAPD also serves as a huge resource to individuals using a service dog through their membership benefits, including discounts on medication and supplies, Pet Assure, and specific vets. Overall, the IAAPD is a large network of service dog support that is continuing to grow in the US and Canada.

Transportation Security Administration (TSA)
Director Office of Civil Rights and Liberties
601 South 12th Street – West Tower, TSA-6
Arlington, Virginia 22202
Attn: External Programs Division
1-866-289-9673
www.tsa.gov
(Updated travel tips. For complaints regarding security checkpoints)

U.S. Department of Transportation (DOT)
Aviation Consumer Protection Division, C-75-D
400 Seventh Street, S.W.
Washington, DC 20590
http://airconsumer.ostdot.gov/escomplaints/es.cfm
(For disability discrimination complaints regarding airlines)

Ridesharing Resources

While the American's with Disabilities Act covers individuals' rights to use and travel with a service dog, some companies have developed supporting policies to curb discrimination within the confines of their platform. Uber and Lyft are two popular platforms used by handlers for travel needs, that have struggled with upholding an accommodating environment for service dogs in the past. Their respective policies can be found here for reference. Please note, both platforms allow for the reporting of service dog related issues within their applications and via their websites.

National Association of Guide Dog User's (NAGDU)
1-813-626-2789
https://www.nagdu.org/

The National Association of Guide Dog Users, (NAGDU,) is a division of the National Federation of the Blind, (NFB,) committed to bringing together guide dog users, puppy raisers, trainers, and anyone wishing to work with guides in these capacities to share access information and advocacy assistance. The NAGDU website has expanded its legislative archives to include access and protection laws from five countries, The United States, Australia, Canada, New Zealand, and The United Kingdom. It is the hopes of this organization to expand the list of service dog related legislation in their archives to many more countries in the future. Members of NAGDU have also developed NAGDU Guide & Service Dog Advocacy Information, an application that allows users to carry the full text of the American's with Disabilities Act, as well as all state statutes pertaining to the rights of service dogs and their handlers in their pocket. General guidance as to public access laws regarding various establishments are also included in this informational application. The app will also connect handlers with advocates who can help pursue and resolve access issues. The app is free on the App Store and is developed by National Association of Guide Dog User's Inc.
www.nagdu.org/nagdu/nagdu-service-dog-app.html
Follow NAGDU on Twitter at @NAGDU, and join the NAGDU support group on Facebook at:
https://m.facebook.com/groups/124908860968667/about/

Uber's Service Animal Policy:
https://accessibility.uber.com/service-animal-policy/

Lyft's Service Animal Policy:
https://help.lyft.com/hc/en-us/articles/115013080048-Service-animal-policy

The National Federation of the Blind entered into landmark settlement agreements with both rideshare companies mentioned above. The settlement required the companies to revise their policies, (listed above,) and to provide additional training for their drivers, and to terminate those drivers that knowingly or repeatedly deny rides to service dog handlers. In an effort to make sure these terms are being met, and to facilitate open communications with both platforms, the NFB asks for service dog users to fill out the following survey to keep up-to-date with customer experiences.
Surveys
https://nfb.org/programs-services/legal-program/uber-and-lyft-survey

Making Life Easier

Blind Travelers Network
https://blindtravelersnetwork.org/

The site provides a wealth of information from experienced blind travelers on their blog and accessible discussion board that allows you to ask questions about places, get tips as a guide dog user and general related information to traveling.

The Independent Airport Traveler; Webinar from Hadley
https://www.hadley.edu/SeminarDetails.asp?sid=170

Great presentation that is full of suggestions for traveling through airports regardless of your approach, using meet and assist services or navigating airports by yourself. The presenter, Jay Stiteley, also provides some great tips for traveling with a guide dog.

Traveling with disabilities
www.Travel.gc.ca
https://travel.gc.ca/travelling/health-safety/disabilities

Where to Go
https://workinglikedogs.com/where-to-go/

This app is free on the App Store and Google Play Store. It provides directions to find relieving areas while traveling through airports. It also provides updates to ADA regulations regarding service animals. Where to Go is developed by Apptology.

Prepare Travels:

Emotional Service Assistance (ESA) / (ACAA)
https://esadoctors.com/airline-requirements-for-traveling-with-an-emotional-support-dog/

Service Dogs and Handlers
1-800-778-4838 (Voice))
1-800-455-9880 (TTY)
www.Tsa.gov

(Air travelers who want information about the rights of person with disabilities in air travel or who experience disability-related air travel service problems may call the Hotline to obtain assistance)

Service Dogs and Animals

Inform the TSA officer that you are traveling with a service animal. You may provide the officer with the TSA notification card or medical documentation to describe your condition.

Screening:
You and your service dog/animal will be screened by a walk-through metal detector. You may walk through together or you may lead the animal through separately on a leash. You will undergo a pat-down if you are not screened by the walk-through metal detector.

If the metal detector alarms, you and/or your service dog/animal will undergo additional screening, including a pat-down.

If the service dog alarms, do not make contact with the dog (other than holding the leash) until the dog has been inspected by an officer. TSA will not separate you from your service animal. If you have concerns about your screening you can ask to speak with a supervisor or passenger support specialist at any point during the process.

Accessories:
Service dog collars, harnesses, leashes, backpacks, vests and other items are subject to screening. Items that are necessary to maintain control of the service dog or indicate that the service dog is on duty do not require removal to be screened.

If you need to relieve your service dog and must exit the security checkpoint, you and the service dog will need to go through the screening process again. You may request to move to the front of the line upon your return.

Medication for service animals must go through X-ray or inspection screening. Separate medications and inform the TSA officer that you carry these items for your service dog.

Flying with your Service Dog

Air travelers who want information about the rights of persons with disabilities in air travel or who experience disability-related air travel service problems may call the Hotline to obtain assistance at:
1-800-778-4838 (voice) or
1-800-455-9880 (TTY).
Accessibility / Canadian Transportation Agency
https://www.otc-cta.gc.ca/eng/accessibility

For disability discrimination complaints regarding airlines:
Send your complaint to:
U.S. Department of Transportation
Aviation Consumer Protection Division , C-75-D
400 Seventh Street, S.W.
Washington, DC 20590

Canadian Flights Complaints
Flights to, from or within Canada
https://services.otc-cta.gc.ca/eng/node/1105

Aviation Consumer Protection Division
Attn: C-75-D
U.S. Department of Transportation
1200 New Jersey Ave, SE
Washington, D.C. 20590
202-366-2220 - (TTY 202-366-0511)
http://airconsumer.ost.dot.gov/escomplaint/es.cfm

For complaints regarding security checkpoints

Department of Homeland Security (DHS)
Office for Civil Rights and Civil Liberties
Mail Stop #0800

245 Murray Lane, S.W.
Building 41
Washington, D.C. 20598

Transportation Security Administration (TSA)
Director, Office of Civil Rights and Liberties
601 South 12th Street – West Tower, TSA-6
Arlington, Virginia 22202
Attn: External Programs Division

Training Schools Links

Assistance Dogs

Autism Assistance Dogs (4 Paws for Ability)
https://4pawsforability.org/autism-assistance-dog/

Canine Companions for Independence (Service Dogs, Facility Dogs, Companion Dogs, Hearing Dogs)
www.cci.org

Dogs with Wings (Service dogs, Autism Dogs, Facility Dogs, and Companion Dogs):
http://dogswithwings.ca

Psychiatric Service Dogs/Mobility Service Dogs (to perform tasks)
https://canines4hope.com/

Diabetic Dogs

Dogs4Diabetics
https://dogs4diabetics.com/

Emotional/Companion Dogs
(Contact your healthcare provider for comfort dogs only)

Facility Dogs

Canine Companion Independence
www.cci.org

Guide Dogs

National Association of Guide Dog Users (Seeing Eye Dogs)
https://www.nagdu.org/nagdu/guide-dog-training-programs.html

Hearing Dogs

Canine Companion Independence (Deaf and Hard of Hearing)
www.cci.org

Dogs for Better Lives: Hearing Dogs
https://dogsforbetterlives.org/hearing-dogs/

Therapy Animals

http://www.therapyanimals.org/.Home/html
http://www.therapyanimals.org/.ITA_Afilliate_Organizations.html

Vet Dogs

Freedom Fidos
www.Freedomfidos.org

We are Here Military
www.operationwearehere.com/MilitaryServiceDogs.html

America's VetDogs
www.Vetdogs.org

Additional Website Links

ADA National Network
https://www.adata.org

Assistance Dog Internations
https://assistancedogsinternational.org/

Freedom Service Dogs of America
https://freedomservicedogs.org/

Service Dogs for America
https://servicedogsforamerica.org/

Wish Upon a Hero
http://www.wishuponahero.com/

Tributes to all Service Dogs

Military Working Dog Teams National Monument
https://en.m.wikipedia.org/wiki/Military_Working)_Do_Teams_N ational_Monument

National Service Animals Monument
https://nationalserviceanimalsmonument.com

War Dogs Memorial
https://en.m.wikipedia.org/wiki/National_War_Dog_Cemetery

US War Dogs Memorial
New Jersey Vietnam Veteran's Memorial
www.njvvmf.org

War Dog Memorial Colorado Spring, Colorado
www.wardogmemorialcolorado.org

US War Dogs Memorial
New Jersey Vietnam Veteran's Memorial
www.njvvmf.org

15 US Dog Memorial Sites to Visit
www.akc.org

LIST OF CONTRIBUTORS
(Alphabetical Order)

Annemarie Agers, Author

Annie Donnell, Author

Aziza Rodriguez, Author

Beth Meador, Author of poem

Billy Vance, Lions Club President.

Boot Sessoms, FF Alumni

Bracha Ben Avraham, Author

Brian McKenna, TSE Trainer

Brian Switzer, Author

Carl Colarusso, FF Alumni

Carolyn Dale Newell, Author

Carrie Ann Musselman, Author

Craig Watford, FF Alumni

Cindy Yorgason, Author

Dan & Bonnie Burgess, D&B Forever

Dave Steele, Author

DeAnna Moore, Author

Disability Law Center

Erica Ihrke, Leader Dogs

Frank Lopez, Author

George Stern, Author

Hampton Sceron, FF Alumni

Holly Bonner, Author

Jackie Hollenbeck, Author

Jane Schlau, Author

Janet Ingber, Author

Jeanette Herbert, First Lady of Utah

Jennifer Bolling, Author

Jopling Family, FF Alumni

Ka Yat Li, Author

Kristin Miller, Author

Kristine Duncan, FF Trainer

Lauren Adams, Author

Lisa Nelson, Library Program Mgr

Matt Burgess, FF Founder

Melvin Reynolds, Author

Patricia Yeager, ILC CEO

Pat Pound, Author

Penny Reeder, GDUI President

Ramona Rice, Book Creator

Randy DeWitt, Editor

Rod Haneline, Leader Dogs

Ronda Del Boccio, Author

Roxanne Bauman, Author

Scott Siegel, Author

Shari Atchison, Author

Shenyo Family, FF Alum

Skye Dunfield, Author

Valerie DePaola, Author

Victoria Heckman, Author

Yvonne Thornton, Author

Made in the USA
Columbia, SC
03 February 2020